Visiting and caring
for the sick

A practical guide
for
relatives, friends and volunteers

Isabelle Delisle
and
Richard Haughian

Visiting and caring
for the sick

A practical guide
for relatives, friends
and volunteers

NOVALIS

Canadian Cataloguing in Publication Data

Delisle Lapierre, Isabelle, 1931-
   Visiting and caring for the sick

   Includes bibliographical references and index.
   ISBN 2-89088-467-8

   1. Church work with the sick. 2. Visiting
the sick. 3. Care of the sick. 4. Sick--Psychology.
I. Haughian, Richard M. II. Title.

BV4335.D4413 1990   259'.4   C90-090544-1

Planning and design committee:

Pierre Bergeron, Director General, Novalis-UniMédia, Montréal

Rev. Donald Bielby, CSC, Director of Pastoral Care and Supervisor of C.P.E. Program,
   Santa Rosa Memorial Hospital, Santa Rosa, California

Rev. Jacques Cloutier, OMI, (formerly Novalis Director)

Rev. Robert Dagenais, Director of Pastoral Care, Hôpital Notre-Dame, Montréal

Sr. Johanne Duggan, SGM, Pastoral Care, Hôpital général de Saint-Boniface, Winnipeg

Jerome Herauf, Novalis editor

Bede Hubbard, Director English language Publishing and Marketing, Novalis-
   UniMédia, Montréal

Sr. Sarah Maillet, RHSJ, Director of Mission Services, Catholic Health Association of
   Canada, Ottawa

Nancy McGee, Spiritual Director, Centre for Spiritual Growth, Ottawa

Revision committee:

Rev. Jacques Cloutier, OMI; Dr. Claude Delisle; Richard Haughian;
   Rev. Normand Provencher, OMI

Illustrations: Gérard Tremblay

Layout and cover design: Gilles Lépine

Cover photo: Karoli Dombi

Copyright © 1990 Novalis, Saint Paul University, Ottawa

Distribution:
Novalis, P.O. Box 990, Outremont, P.Q. H2V 4S7

ISBN: 2-89088-467-8

Printed in Canada

NOVALIS

Contents

Introduction

In recent years the practice of visiting sick persons has markedly increased in popularity. A growing number of hospitals and homes for chronic or nursing care have organized groups of volunteers who regularly visit those who are sick. Many parishes and congregations have established their own pastoral care teams whose members visit in health care institutions and at home. Team members minister to sick people by offering them the compassion and support of the Christian community and, often, by bringing them the Eucharist.

Those engaged in this ministry need to renew themselves on a regular basis to ensure that their service continues to be effective. Relatives and friends can also improve the quality of their care for their loved ones by learning appropriate attitudes, successful interventions and behaviour to be avoided.

This guide is intended for relatives, friends and volunteers as a practical introduction to assisting sick people in the specific circumstances of their illness. It is meant to help care-givers be present with them in a spirit of compassion and mutual search for spiritual growth.

Those who are sick are very dependent on the persons who care for them. They must constantly adjust to the circumstances of their illness and to the treatments they receive. Their distinctive personalities determine, to a great extent, how they respond to these situations and co-operate with the care they receive. Care-givers must strive, therefore, to be familiar with the unique characteristics and conditions of the particular sick persons they are visiting.

Visitors should learn certain important skills if they wish to be able to meet people who are suffering at their point of need. They must first develop a great capacity for hearing the feelings lived and expressed by the sick person. They can then learn specific ways of responding that assist the ailing in freeing themselves from those feelings that are stifling them. Visitors should strive to become adept at using behaviour and gestures that are appropriate to the needs of the sick at any particular moment.

Visitors, finally, also have to learn how to relate with other care-givers, hospital personnel, relatives, friends and volunteers, so that together they can create a peaceful and comfortable atmosphere that facilitates physical, mental and spiritual health.

Spiritual accompaniment is an important service offered by visiting care-givers, when sick people themselves express a desire for it. They can help to arrange a visit by a member of the clergy requested, and they must be sensitive to the wishes of those who prefer confidentiality on this point.

Visiting care-givers need to know how to communicate a realistic sense of hope, being attentive to the signs of life that reveal themselves in the trials and difficulties experienced by the sick. These care-givers will thus be able, finally, to help those who are ill to search for their own source of peace in the face of what the future may bring.

May this book be an inspiration and guide for all those who have chosen to take up this special ministry of visiting and caring for the sick person.

Part one

Knowledge of sick people and their needs

Chapter one

The stresses of being sick

Different degrees of sickness

Dependency

Pain

Suffering

Sickness profoundly changes the lives of those who are sick: immobility that can be more or less total, pain, sorrow, complicated treatments, and often a dislocation in every aspect of their lives. These changes affect their lifestyle and the social milieu to which they have been accustomed since childhood.

Different degrees of sickness

We must understand from the beginning that there are diverse kinds of sicknesses with different degreees of difficulty and stress.

1.   Sicknesses that can be cured. A person enters a hospital for a treatment or operation, confident of an early recovery. After a certain period of time, the length depending on the medical condition, the person returns to his or her ordinary life with few after-effects from the sickness. With such a sick person, contacts are usually easy, resembling the warm visits of good friends.

2.   Chronic illnesses. These are long, incurable illnesses that do not cause death but often have the effect of years of pain, restricted movement and anxiety about the future. Those who suffer from these illnesses become bored and discouraged, especially if they are immobilized. They need regular, friendly visits. Visitors ought to encourage them to be concerned about others, if they can—to comfort those suffering from the same condition as they are.

3.   Terminal illnesses. When those who are sick see clearly that there is no hope of recovery, when they understand that death is imminent, they need to express these feelings, to be assured of the support of a faithful and loving presence that can help them to find meaning in their suffering and death. This last stage of life can sometimes be truly blessed when it is lived in a spirit of faith and hope.

Of all the hardships that sickness causes, the condition of dependency is probably the hardest to bear and one that people never really completely accept.

"I discovered the extraordinary importance of dependency some years ago in a hospital. I was seriously sick, unable to leave my bed or even to move, except for turning on my side.

"In this extreme condition of helplessness I learned how much we need other people. This is a need not only for chief physicians and their interns, for day and night nurses, but also for volunteer care-givers. They are needed for the treatment they provide as well as for their acts of kindness and words of encouragement... And, then, the expectation of visits from family and friends is so important. On leaving the hospital, I had become convinced that dependency is a permanent given in the life of the sick" (Albert Memmie, *La dépendance*, p.258).

Although those who are bedridden require more assistance than those who are mobile, they have not lost their ability to express their needs. Their wishes and decisions are to be listened to and respected.

The stresses of dependency arise from a radical role change. Sick persons, often quite suddenly, find themselves forced to take on an unaccustomed role. The mother of a family, for example, who has taken care of her children for so many years now finds herself in the unusual position of being cared for by others, even by her own children.

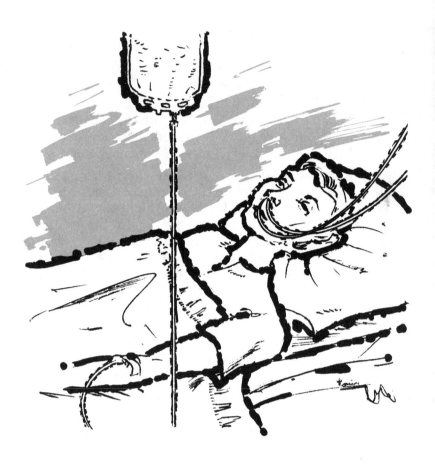

Such a role reversal can be very stressful, especially if the sick have linked their identity or sense of self-worth to what they do, i.e. caring for others, rather than to who they are.

Pain

Let us distinguish between pain and suffering. Pain is an unpleasant sensation felt in one part of the body; suffering is an enduring emotion felt more on the psychological and spiritual levels of one's being.

Suffering results from a complex of factors that combine to render one's life more and more difficult, and even at times unbearable. The support of family, friends and volunteers will respond most frequently to the needs of sick persons on the level of their suffering.

Pain manifests itself in different ways, from muscle discomfort to acute cases of arthritis or cardiac infarction. The body itself naturally manufactures hormones giving partial immunization to pain. An example of this is the secretion of cerebral hormones called "endorphines." Modern medicine has successfully learned to reduce physical pain through the use of drugs that range from aspirin to derivatives of opium. Because of this, those who are seriously sick can now be assured that their pain can be reasonably controlled.

Suffering

Suffering amplifies and intensifies the many physical pains the sick person must endure. It adds the dehumanizing feeling of dependency, the irritations and resentments caused by repeated treatments, worry about loved ones, anxiety about the future, the tediousness of inactivity and loneliness, and questions of meaning and purpose.

All of these factors taken together can result, at times, in an extreme state that perhaps can be called a "pain sickness." This consists of a body reaction to overwhelming moral suffering.

Suffering reflects one's personality

The same objective pains can have different effects on different individuals, depending upon their temperaments and characters. In other words, some people feel physical pain more because they are more sensitive, more focussed on their own ills, less hardened against the difficulties of life.

Physical pain can sometimes be so great that it totally monopolizes one's attention. Dr. René Leriche, author, has observed cases of this kind: "In a very short time, pain can turn the most radiant spirit into a hunted being, turned in on itself, fixated on its illness, indifferent to everyone and everything

else, totally obsessed by fear that the pain will return." (*La chirurgie de la douleur*, Masson, Paris, 1937)

Those overwhelmed by extreme pain become defenceless, thrown back on their physical needs, even in an immoderate way, as if nothing else existed. Their consciousness is completely preoccupied and blocked by the feeling of suffering, which even increases their agony.

Others manage to escape this vicious circle, apart from moments of crisis. They have learned to direct their attention to social or religious activities, or to other interesting aspects of their lives.

A therapy for suffering

It is important to create a supportive atmosphere for the sick person in areas of ordinary life. Suffering is more bearable, it seems, when material circumstances are agreeable, attractive to the eye, and when those who are sick are surrounded by friends who know them and show them their affection. Family, friends and volunteers play a crucial role in these extremely difficult moments of sickness.

Psychiatry, hypnotherapy and sophrology (the study of interior harmony) can be very useful in helping those who are ailing to divert their attention from their illness. This can be done, for example, by consciously attending to other things like a beautiful scene, or by the systematic relaxation of each part of the body. Therapies and techniques such as these can complement medication in reducing the pain and suffering, thus making their lives less burdensome.

Finding meaning in suffering

In an even more profound way, it is possible to find meaning in suffering and to learn how to integrate it into one's life. For those who cherish spiritual goals, suffering can be a passage to deeper personal truth, and a way of drawing closer to the mystery of God's love. The power of suffering is the same in one's life as the power of loving. With the help of grace, unavoidable suffering can be welcomed as a visit from God who invites the sick person to abandon herself or himself into God's hands.

Few of us, perhaps, will arrive at such a point of abandonment. But those who are sick can strive, with the help of prayer and the support of friends who share the same spiritual goals, to find meaning in the pains and sufferings of their lives.

Chapter two

Different categories of sickness

The demanding-dependent

The orderly-controlled

The dramatic-emotive

The hypochondriac

The passive-aggressive

The unstable

When people become sick their personalities do not change, but temperament and character traits that before the illness had been little noticed become accentuated.

Physicians usually classify their patients according to specific categories or personality types. We are borrowing here the classification of (two medical doctors practising in Hull, Quebec) Doctor Jean-Pierre Bernatchez, psychiatrist, as recommended by Doctor Claude Delisle for his students. He uses the following categories:

the demanding-dependent

the orderly-controlled

the dramatic-emotive

the hypochondriac

the passive-aggressive

the unstable

We must remember that many of these traits are found, in different degrees, in everyone who is sick. There is no such person, for example, as a pure hypochondriac. It is the emphasis that changes in each case.

We will briefly describe each of these categories and recommend attitudes and behaviour that are appropriate for health-care personnel and visitors.

To begin this section with a bit of humour, I would encourage you, the reader, to try to apply this range of categories to yourself to see which fits best!

The demanding-dependent

These people demand a lot of attention. They fear being abandoned, yet, in order to attract attention to themselves, sometimes go to the extent of rejecting care. They are inclined to anger, to continuous complaining and to depression. In a word, they demand constant attention, like a child.

Our attitude

Care-givers should give these patients the same care as given to others, explaining to them kindly but firmly the limits that must be imposed on their demands. No attempt should be made to change their personality when they are in an acute stage, but an effort can be made to help them to mature psychologically.

Visits should not be too long, so as not to encourage these persons to become too dependent on the care-givers. Visitors should know how to dedicate that quality and quantity of attention to those who are ill that they are capable of giving. In summary, visiting care-givers should assume the same attitudes that they might have for a child who is somewhat unpredictable.

The orderly-controlled

These people are very meticulous, sticklers for details, scrupulous and disciplined. But they are obstinate and wish to control situations to the point of humiliating themselves. They make redoubled efforts, therefore, to keep as much control over their treatment as they can.

Our attitude

The health-care team is to inform patients about their illness in a clear and precise manner. The team can allow them to collaborate in their treatment by letting them choose, if it is convenient, the times for taking their medication. They can also be invited to draw up the list of symptoms they have observed during the development of their illness. Such initiatives will give them confidence in their capacities, and their collaboration will improve their progress.

Visiting care-givers should listen patiently to patients' detailed descriptions of the history of their sickness and of the treatments they have received. Through active listening they can help them to express their feelings and fears. A rational and objective approach does not suffice. These people also need to verbalize their feelings and to free themselves from their fears.

The dramatic-emotive

These people are very emotionally involved because their sickness seems to them to be a defect, a personal failure. They take great pains to be admired and esteemed in spite of their illness. They have a tendency to become intensely involved with others, with the unconscious need to be admired.

Our attitude

Care-givers can reassure the sick by giving them explanations, but without going into many details. They might have to repeat these explanations several times, since these persons are accustomed to nod agreement without really hearing what has been said to them.

Visiting care-givers should be reassuring and supportive. They should listen to patients' complaints and, through prolonged visits, help them to ventilate their deeply-felt emotions. They must know how to keep a healthy balance between being too close or too distant.

The hypochondriac

Hypochondriacs are characterized by their excessive concern about the state of their health even when they are well. If they ever do become sick, they keep demanding repeated tests and new treatments. They go from one physician to another, from one treatment or technique to another, even from one charlatan to another, always remaining anxious when someone tries to reassure them.

Our attitude

The medical team has to acknowledge that these people need to be sick, and to patiently accept listening to the enumeration of their many symptoms. They should never promise a cure or even an improvement in their condition, because it seems that these people need to believe that they are sick.

Visitors should listen attentively to patients' unending complaints. They must strive to be empathic at all times, since these people have a great need for love and esteem.

The passive-aggressive

These patients resist advice offered to them, but in a passive way without openly opposing it. They tend to blame others for what happens to them. They appear externally to accept what others suggest to them, though internally they reject it.

Our attitude

The medical team does well to avoid an authoritarian style of relating that would spark the internal resistance typical of these people. They seek instead to emphasize adult-adult relationships between patients and care-givers, in order to go beyond these rebellious attitudes.

Visitors should allow the sick to express openly their hesitations, their lack of confidence. By their attitude of acceptance, visitors perhaps can help patients to discover and trust the competence and good intentions of the health-care team. They must try also to avoid authoritarian and protective attitudes that encourage the passive resistance reactions of this personality type.

The unstable

These patients could be referred to as borderline or unstable—that is, on the edge of very serious character problems. Their moods are unpredictable; they can easily pass from uncontrolled anger to compliments and to lies. Certain alcoholics and narcomaniacs exhibit the same traits.

Our attitude

Care-givers need to be consistent in their attitudes and behaviour. They must know how to set and maintain clearly defined limits with the purpose of insuring regular and attentive care. Attention to the medication dosage is particularly important since these patients have a pressing need to receive their customary drugs.

Visitors must be careful to resist the patients' requests for alcohol, drugs or other non-prescribed medication. They do well to consult with the physician, psychiatrist or psychiatric nurse for the best attitude and behaviour to adopt with particularly difficult patients. Very often they have to combine kindness with firmness in order to avoid being manipulated and destabilizing the patients' condition.

In the face of these complex human situations, care-givers must be careful not to make superficial and malicious judgments. Those who are sick, with their own temperaments and characters, have been affected by family experiences and childhood traumas. When they are in great suffering, their survival instinct pushes them to turn in on themselves to concentrate all of their energy on their illness. And it sometimes happens that the darker tendencies of their personalities reveal themselves.

Visiting care-givers are encouraged to make a special effort to understand well the psychological and social systems that have helped to shape the lives of those they are visiting. Only through such understanding will they be able to hear and respond to the needs of sick persons, and in this way to contribute to their well-being at these critical moments of their lives.

Chapter three

Being sick
and the process
of adapting to it

A person's needs in times of sickness

The experience of sickness

Living in the present

Attention to the personal dimension of a person's immediate surroundings enhances the quality of his or her experience of life. For the sick person this personal dimension consists of the type of treatment received, the kindness of the health-care personnel and the support of visitors.

The quality of this milieu greatly affects a person's hopes, plans and happiness.

A person's needs in times of sickness

In stressful situations the body adapts by transforming itself. This truth is well illustrated by the example of a tree. When a branch breaks, the tree does not restore itself by grow-

ing another branch in the same place, but by a reorganizing of its whole structure.

The same thing occurs when someone becomes ill. The return to health requires an adaptation of the entire person to the new circumstances of his or her situation.

Needs that are specific to the sick

The fundamental needs of the human person always remain the same. And in ordinary circumstances, if these basic needs are not satisfied, the body suffers serious consequences. But in times of sickness these needs take on a new meaning because the sickness creates its own specific problems.

A person, for example, who has suffered a fractured hip will require a long period of rehabilitation and assistance in order to move about.

Because of the inactivity brought on by his illness, a man feels that he is useless and of little value. He will need someone to help him to become more aware of his personal worth so that he can feel useful again.

A woman, due to her sickness, is unable to take up again her role as mother. She will want support from her family to deal

26

with the anguish she feels, faced with the responsibities she can no longer assume.

In their work, *Alors survint la maladie* ["When sickness occurs"], the group of researchers known as SIRIM (Société Internationale de Recherche Interdisciplinaire sur la Maladie) state that a human being has three essential needs: the need to act, the need to have personal space, and the need to achieve social fulfillment. These needs take on added significance during times of illness.

The need to act

As human beings we live in a milieu that is both social and physical. Coping with this milieu is never easy. Life is full of problems and we must take action to solve them if we are going to survive.

We function from the "fight or flight" principle. When confronted with difficulties we can choose either to confront the situation or to run from it. These are the two possible action responses that allow us to survive. If we can neither confront nor run away, we remain stuck, prisoners of the situation.

At one moment we ought to adjust to the situation; at another time, we should take the circumstances in hand and change them.

This is the predicament of sick persons. How can they adapt to their condition of illness? Yet how can they change it? If they are unable to act, their condition risks deterioration.

Awareness of this fundamental human need to act can help those who are sick to find their path to healing. And care-givers will be, at times, a mirror, enabling them to find within themselves the energy to act, according to their own capacities.

The need for personal space

A sense of territory is not an arbitrary value. It is found among animals as well as among human beings. Those who have domestic animals know this well.

Animals that are deprived of their own territory can fall sick and die. Human beings likewise need their own space in order to perform their proper activities and to grow.

Personal territory includes home environment, work, children, leisure, etc. If one of these vital areas becomes neglected, life loses its sense of equilibrium.

Someone who undergoes a prolonged period of hospitalization loses this sense of equilibrium. When this happens the sick person often loses the desire and even the capacity to fight back, little by little giving in to the illness.

To have one's personal space is to have the capacity to act in an autonomous manner. Care-givers can help those who are sick by encouraging them to be independent to the extent that their condition allows.

Personal space and readiness to fight are inextricably linked together. The capacity to act independently enables a person

to survive;

to stand up for personal integrity;

to provide his or her comfort and security;

to achieve personal growth.

The need for social fulfillment

An action may be finished, but it is not complete until it has attained its original goal. The condition of someone who has attempted to do something and failed can be worse than that of one who has not tried to do anything at all.

The birth of a child, for example, which is the normal completion of nine months' pregnancy, is the fulfillment of a long waiting period. If the child should die at birth, however, the mother feels, in addition to the pain of loss, a sense of social deprivation.

A young engineer has found a good job where he can put his recently acquired knowledge to good use. His long years of study have reached their expected fulfillment. His goal has been achieved. This same young man, after a medical examination, learns that he has cancer. We can imagine the intensity of his reaction to this news.

We all react in our own distinctive way to the setbacks of life or to the distressing occurrence of serious illness. But, whoever we are, we will all need support from others to pass through this period of crisis.

Moments of crisis always disorient us. But they can be necessary at certain moments in our lives if we want to know ourselves better and to take greater responsibility for ourselves. Such events will not be experienced as alien to us if we have learned how to understand them in light of our own personal evolution.

Sickness brings with it many changes that often force us to give up our protective shell. It shatters the restrictive mold within which we have shaped our lives in conformity with the norms of our culture and the expectations of our friends and acquaintances.

We are shocked to discover that the beautiful image we had of ourselves is an illusion. And this false identity must die if our true self is to live.

Can we not find, then, with the help of a friend, some benefits in being sick?

Sickness can cause in us a profound personal crisis. We can feel threatened, immobilized for a time, overcome by fear.

Illness is usually the bearer of unforeseen events that disorient our lives, throwing us into a state of utter vulnerability.

In this situation we can withdraw into ourselves and become depressed. Or we can mobilize our energies to seek a solution to our problems, and in so doing to give a new meaning to our lives.

Sickness inevitably changes our lives. This change can be positive if it helps us to deepen our freedom and autonomy, to become aware that we are entirely responsible for ourselves. We are the only ones ultimately who can take care of ourselves.

Becoming responsible for ourselves means being able to face the chance mishaps we call accidents, sickness, misfortunes—and seeking in these events our own unique answers.

Is it not at the price of our losses that we grow in freedom and inner strength? The changes brought on by illness can lead us to a new vision of life, to an awareness of a part of ourselves that has been stifled by superficial activities, and to a changed direction for our lives.

Sickness is a reminder of the temporary quality of all things. This realization can help those who are sick to discover in their illness an important message: if being sick is an experience of limitation, hardship and deprivation, it is also, very often, an opportunity to learn more about our real selves.

Every experience that has not revealed something better has yet to achieve its full meaning. For many people sickness is such a passage toward personal fulfillment.

An attitude of acceptance can enable those who are sick to go beyond themselves, to transcend their being. This deepening sense of detachment will allow them to live in peace and serenity and to adjust to the changes that illness brings.

We will never adjust to sickness without learning how "to live in the present."

"To live in the present" is to live each moment to its fullness without being attached either to the past or to the future. The past is over; the future is not yet ours.

You may rightly say that this is not the easiest thing to do. But it is the only way we have of preserving our inner equilibrium, of being present to what is happening now and of being attentive to what is to come.

Is not life a journey, a journey into an unknown country where each step brings its own surprise? On this journey we can learn so much about ourselves, about those with whom we travel, about the world we see around us.

Often the illness itself is not that negative. Rather, it is our attitude toward the illness that can either destroy us or lead us to new stages of growth.

Fear is often our number one enemy preventing us from living in the present. Fear distorts our perceptions and provokes constrained reactions that lead us into a state of anxiety. When fear enters our hearts, happiness, courage and peace are driven away.

Our fearful thoughts affect our minds, our bodies and our spirits. They also affect the state of other beings living around us. Like vibrating antennas, others pick up the positive and negative waves that radiate from us.

If we were convinced that what happens to us in every circumstance is always for the best, we would more easily live in the present moment. Our refusal to live in the present is a refusal to face reality, a saying no to growth and to the enjoyment of true freedom. The wise person is free because she or he wants only what in fact happens. Nothing can take away this interior freedom.

For the Christian, faith reaches even greater depths in the certitude of divine love. With St. Paul, we profess that God co-operates with all those who love God, turning everything into good. (*Romans* 8:28).

My prayer is a cry bursting forth from my deepest being. It is a beggar's glance; a bruised spirit; an adventure of total abandonment into the hands of the All-Powerful.

My prayer is a certitude that He exists despite every affliction; a certitude that one day a great light will dissipate the shadows. My prayer is the belief that a time of pain is a time of grace and a step closer to the Absolute.

Marie-Cécile Généreux

Chapter four

Sick persons
in the role of care-givers

Sick persons as instructors

Sick persons as partners

The care-giver as a mirror for those who are sick

The losses experienced during an illness can lead those who are ill to become very critical of those around them. They can even build a wall between themselves and their care-givers. How does this happen?

Because people who are sick have their own frame of reference, they can resist the imposition of other points of view. They feel a need to have some control over their lives, to be the ones to take stock of their own condition, to assess the state of their health and progress. The role of their care-givers is to provide them with the support and comfort they need, to affirm their strengths and to call them to a sense of their own independence.

This support is indispensable. But the interventions of care-givers risk being inappropriate if those who are sick do not actually experience themselves as givers and helpers of others.

It is in this sense that people who are sick are at once instructors and partners of their care-givers.

Sick persons as instructors

What can sick persons teach us?

– They can help us to question our priorities.

– They prod us on to discover the meaning of our lives.

– They teach us the spirit of detachment.

– They reveal to us the joy of living.

Our priorities

Those who are ill can give us—we who are "in good health"—the courage to question ourselves, to evaluate our priorities.

If we find life hard, are annoyed by the demands of our daily routine, complain of all the obstacles that upset our plans, then a glance at a sick person may perhaps speak volumes to us.

Many of our own sufferings seem light when placed next to the overwhelming losses that others carry.

Because they live in this condition minute by minute, sick persons can help us to face our own daily reality. They witness to the need to live in the present, one day at a time, for the anticipation of tomorrow can be for them a source of stress and anxiety.

The meaning of life

Illness leads those who are sick to reassess their lives. What does this illness say to them about the way they've lived their lives? Have they lived with too much stress? Have they en-couraged destructive habits? Have they not known how to respect their proper limits?

And what about ourselves? Perhaps we have also lived with too much stress. Are some of our habits destructive, etc.?

We can learn from sick persons a wiser perspective on the consumer society that envelops us. We can learn that life is a series of personal choices and decisions. If we do not want to be victims, we must take possession of our lives with full aware-ness of the choices we make.

In this way we can experience ourselves becoming truly free. Those who are sick confront us with the truth, our own

32

truth: what are the barriers preventing us from growing physically, psychologically and spiritually? Will we wait until we ourselves are ill in order to reflect on our lifestyle?

The necessity of detachment

Sickness inevitably brings with it many losses. Those afflicted have had to deal with being separated from work and, if hospitalized, being absent from home, spouse, children and friends. And for how long a time?

They must learn to transform these hurts and other negative forces into positive energy that can be mobilized to deal constructively with their illness.

Contact with sick persons invites us, likewise, to go beyond ourselves, to take the same positive attitude to the negative influences in our own lives. It teaches us to say goodbye to the persons and things that we love.

Detachment involves a letting go of what is secure and familiar, a difficult period of weaning much like the infant learning to eat solid food. It can be a time of frustration, emptiness, almost despair.

Yet for many people these losses due to illness are the beginning of greater maturity in detachment.

The joy of living

Life, the simple fact of being alive, takes on an added importance when our bodies are racked by pain. Everything else seems unimportant! What would we not give then to have our health back?

If we but let ourselves gaze upon the life of someone who is sick, would not our easy certitudes and priorities be questioned?

When we are bored by life and overcome by inertia, the presence of others who are suffering might be enough to shake us from our complacency. To take up the struggle again, to see life once more as an opportunity instead of as a problem, to rediscover our sense of wonder instead of complaining and always demanding more from life. Then we can exclaim with the psalmist that our hearts are full of joy because we have been set free (Psalm 13:5).

These are the important lessons of life that sick people can teach us. Such experiences have led Elizabeth Kübler-Ross, that outstanding woman who has taught us so much about caring for dying persons, to say that her patients have been her best instructors, her masters.

A partner is someone with whom we are associated for a particular reason. Unlike the relationship with a parent or a close friend, the partner relationship is the type that the care-giver will try to establish with the sick person. To be a partner the care-giver must look for the right balance between identification with, and distance from, the sick person.

When we identify with another, we enter into their feelings. If done without detachment and respect, this can prevent the care-giver from fulfilling his or her proper role. To allow ourselves to be overwhelmed by the feelings of another, for example, is to relate to that person more out of sympathy than out of empathy. But let us explain this more fully.

Empathy

Empathy is the capacity to share another's experience while remaining emotionally free in the relationship. It comes from an inner security that allows the care-giver to face unexpected and distressing events with emotional equilibrium.

Such care-givers can establish authentic and personal relationships with others because of their goodness, sense of responsibility and objective interest. They feel emotionally at ease with themselves. They are capable, therefore, of entering without fear into an affective relationship that is both deeply emotional and secure.

What then characterizes the care-giver/receiver of care relationship? It is a relationship of friendship, gratuitous love, confidence and a certain mutual support. The one who gives receives as much, if not more, than the one who receives.

It is always a matter of enabling those receiving the care to become conscious of their own resources, of the ability they have to understand the origins of their problems and to solve these by themselves.

By their repeated visits, the care-givers acquire a sufficient understanding of those they are visiting, their frame of mind, their conscious and unconscious needs. They know how to maintain a distance so as not to become engulfed by the other's subjective world.

From their more objective perspective, care-givers will be able to tell the sick, if the occasion arises, that the solutions are not always very simple and that many outside factors influence their lives.

Being a partner of those who are sick

Being a partner of sick persons requires an interior stability and psychological maturity. Carl Rogers, psychologist, has written (*Le développement de la personne*) that our capacity to create relationships that will facilitate another person's growth to independence is determined by our own level of growth.

The spirit of partnership is accompaniment, not guidance. We will see in a later chapter how active listening is both an attitude and a technique for helping others to believe in themselves, to take greater responsibility for their own lives and to settle their own problems with our assistance.

Why avoid sympathy?

Sympathy is an instinctive fondness that attracts two people to each other. This type of feeling typically exists between two members of the same family or two close friends.

When sympathy exists between a woman who is sick and a female relative, for example, the relative might say: "It is so difficult for me to help her; I am too close to her and I feel too deeply all that she feels." This person is engulfed by the feelings of the woman she loves.

This sick person, on the other hand, may not share what she is feeling with those she loves lest she bring them more suffering. But she may be comfortable talking with an outsider, with someone who could be described as a care-giver. With this person she might be free to share all that she is feeling because the other is a partner in this relationship and not an intimate. Theirs is an empathic relationship characterized by positive feelings of acceptance, respect and even friendship.

Empathy means understanding the sick person without feeling pity for him or her. One can help those who are afflicted to carry their suffering, by attitudes of listening and understanding, without assuming an attitude connoted by the word "sympathy." Understanding and support do not imply pity.

The care-giver as a mirror for those who are sick

A mirror reflects an object or person; it picks up an image and places it before our eyes. Those who are ill need to see themselves in the eyes of another, to see their suspicions confirmed, to find the truth of their situation. They look to their care-givers to be this mirror for them.

But this role is difficult for care-givers. Are we not all influenced by our past experiences? If we have been traumatized by certain medical treatments, will we easily accept that the sick person is undergoing these same treatments? Take someone who has cancer and has been prescribed chemotherapy. Or if we have exaggerated fears—of AIDS, for example—will we not project this fear on the sick person?

Two pitfalls can prevent care-givers from playing a mirror role: projection and transference.

What is projection?

The word "projection" comes from psychoanalysis. It is a psychological mechanism by which we attribute to another our own feelings and motivations.

If, for example, we are accompanying someone who is dying and we do not accept death ourselves, we might tend to say to this person "Don't give up," because of our own denial of death.

What then can be done? Ideally, care-givers ought to be able:

- to recognize a situation for what it is without projecting on it personal wishes, fantasies or fears;

- to describe the situation accurately;

- to identify the emotions and reactions the situation has evoked in themselves, and to accept them without denying

36

or seeking to avoid them;

- to accept the situation for what it is, at the moment, even though wanting to change it in the future if the occasion arises;

- to express to others (who are directly or emotionally involved in the situation) their perceptions and personal reactions.

Understandably, we rarely respond ideally. When we have difficulty communicating with a sick person, one of the first questions to ask ourselves is: at what level is the difficulty?

It could be:

- a difficulty forming a clear image of the situation;

- a difficulty getting in touch with the feelings and interior reactions the situation evokes;

- a difficulty accepting the situation and the reactions for what they are in the present moment;

- a difficulty obtaining information from those directly involved, or being late in obtaining it.

Once we have identified the difficulty, we will more easily be able to choose the appropriate intervention for overcoming it.

What is transference?

Care-givers, acting as mirrors of those who are ill, can bring about a transference whereby the latter see in them their own grandfather, mother, sister, brother, etc.

Transference, in psychoanalysis, refers to a group of reactions whereby someone transforms personal fantasies and conflicts by projecting them onto the person before him or her.

A nurse working in palliative care confided to me that she relived the death of her mother each time a patient died. Another nurse spoke of the grief she experienced at the loss of each patient.

How many people have been forced by burnout to leave their work because the sight of so many sick people became unbearable? They were seeing loved ones in all the sick persons they were serving.

Too often we want to carry the other. We insist on the will to live when it is really time to let go. Fear of not doing enough often directs our actions. We feel guilty for the sick person's illness and death.

By paying attention to these transferences in our relationships, we will more easily free ourselves from false guilt feelings in many difficult situations.

To be present with those who are sick is emotionally draining. To do this on a regular basis, care-givers need an equilibrium in their own lives. In order to maintain their own good physical and mental health, they must have life-giving activities apart from their care-giving involvement with others.

Part two

Assisting those who are sick

Chapter five

Personal hygiene

The regular bath

Preparation for the bath

Special baths

Care of the mouth

Care of the hair

Care of the nails

Care of the skin and bed sores

Care of the sick person always includes a program of good personal hygiene. Specific measures vary with the physical and psychological conditions of those who are ill.

Age is one factor to consider in matters of personal hygiene. An elderly man, for example, does not need to have a complete bath every day, since this practice could excessively dry out his skin and cause cracks, due to the loss of natural body oils and the decrease of perspiration.

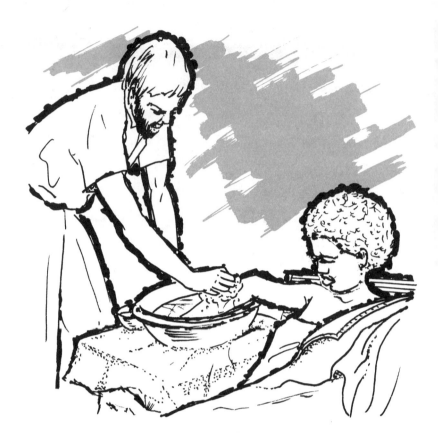

A young person, on the other hand, needs a daily bath. This can also be for her or him a moment of extraordinary relaxation, an opportunity for personal human contact.

The suggestions offered here apply especially to care of those sick at home. The professional staff of hospitals and residences usually take care of the personal hygienic needs of the sick person. Volunteers should respond to these needs only with the approval of personnel responsible for patient or resident care.

The regular bath

Bathing brings comfort to the sick person and contributes to physical, emotional and mental well-being.

Regular baths have specific goals:

- to clean the skin;
- to remove organic waste;
- to stimulate circulation of the blood;
- to refresh the person.

We will speak first of bathing in bed, which is done with a washcloth or a soft sponge.

Turning the person in bed

It is easy for one person to turn the sick person by using the following instructions:

– approach the sick person from one side of the bed;

– place their upper knee in the direction of the intended movement and bend their leg so that the foot rests on the lower knee;

– place their arm along their body in such a way that they can turn by rolling over the arm;

– grab hold of their shoulder with one hand and their hip with the other and push firmly. The person will turn easily from one side to the other.

Suggestions for bathing in bed

The water temperature should be about 40°C (in other words, slightly higher than normal body temperature).

Wash the entire body beginning with the face, then the arms, the chest, the stomach, the genital organs and the legs. Turn the person and do the same with the back.

It is important to uncover only that part of the body that is being washed. Sometimes they will prefer to wash their own genitals, so offer them this possibility if they are able.

After the bath a good rubdown, especially of the back, is very comforting for someone who is ill.

The sponge bath is used to lower the person's temperature and to reduce tension. Add a bit of rubbing alcohol to the water to increase evaporization and to help the person to cool down. Take her or his temperature before the bath and 30 minutes later to check the results.

Bathing is a good therapy—physically, psychologically and spiritually. It is during the relaxed atmosphere of a bath that a person may frequently wish to talk and to confide his or her anxieties and difficulties.

A nurse once told me that the best moment of the day was bath time. The benefit that it brought to the sick person flowed over and increased her own joy.

Preparation for the bath

Check that the temperature of the room is warm enough (about 24-25°C). Those who are sick and elderly persons need a higher temperature. Avoid drafts even in the summer.

Place all the items needed for the bath on the bedside table, including those required for oral care.

Raise the head of the bed, if this is possible.

Materials required:

- a basin of warm water (around 40°C);
- gentle soap;
- two washcloths and two towels;
- a large towel to place under the limbs;
- clean bedding;
- clean clothes;
- a bag for soiled linen.

Special baths

We speak here of complete baths in which the body is immersed in water up to the neck. For those who are disabled,

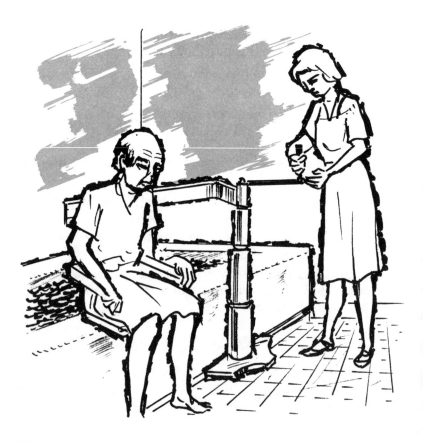

two persons are needed to put them into the bath, although it is possible to obtain lifting devices that are completely safe.

Baths of relaxation

A bath, generally speaking, ought not to last longer than 15 to 20 minutes, especially if the water is warm. For a regular bath, a temperature of 40°C would be considered normal. Hot water baths (43 to 45°C) help to lessen muscle discomfort and pain.

Whirlpool baths give the body a gentle massage. They help to reduce tension and have a calming effect on the body.

Some additives to the water produce beneficial effects, both physically and psychologically. Starch, bicarbonate of soda and oats are good examples.

To add starch: dilute one-half kilogram of starch in cold water; add some hot water; bring to a boil for two minutes on a low flame; mix into bath water.

To add bicarbonate of soda: dissolve a teaspoon of soda in one-half litre of warm water; mix into bath water.

To add oats: put three cups of ordinary oats in two litres of water; heat until consistency is thick and pasty; place in a piece of gauze and stir in bath water.

Stimulating baths

For some people who are sick, a bath with sea water or with mustard can be pleasant and stimulating for the skin.

To add sea water: dissolve one teaspoon of sea salt in one-half litre of water; pour into bath water.

To add mustard: dilute one tablespoon of dry mustard in four litres of lukewarm water (for children, use one-half tablespoon); mix into bath water (the temperature of the bath water should be about 36°C).

Soaking baths

Soaking has remarkable therapeutic value because it removes dead tissue from the body and helps the suppuration of wounds. For the latter purpose, carefully follow the physician's instructions about the solution to use, the temperature of the water and the frequency of the soakings. Bath seats are often used after rectal and vaginal surgery and after delivery.

Place the following items on a table: a toothbrush with toothpaste, a glass of water, a small basin, and a denture container if required.

Wet the toothbrush and apply the toothpaste. Let those who are sick brush their own teeth if they can. If they are unable to sit, have them turn their head to your side and place a towel under their chin. For the rinse put a curved basin under their mouth, then wipe their face with a towel.

If they are handicapped or unconscious, proceed in the same manner but use very little water for the rinse. To clean the back of the mouth, the palate and the tongue, use an applicator saturated with glycerine and lemon. Then rinse.

To wash dentures, use ordinary methods. Commercial solutions can be used for soaking them during the night.

Care of the hair

Shampooing the hair is usually done during a bath. To shampoo those who are in bed, place a plastic cover and towel under their head. Wet their hair with a small amount of lukewarm water, taking care not to let the water flow into their eyes or ears or onto their face.

It helps to put a facecloth over their eyes to protect them from soap.

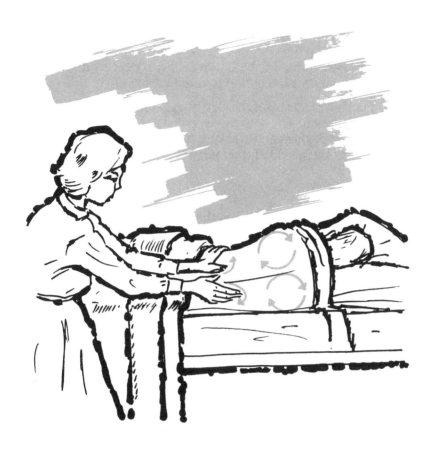

Apply a small amount of shampoo and vigorously massage the scalp. Rinse with care. Dry the hair, neck and ears, using a hair dryer as needed.

To comb long hair, place your hand between the scalp and the hair ends. Begin by brushing the ends, then gently move back toward the roots. Encourage those who are sick to do their own hair if they can, and offer to hold the mirror for them.

Care of the nails

Bath time is also the best time for cutting the nails. Before doing this for elderly persons, soak their nails in warm water for about 10 minutes, since their nails are dry and brittle.

Care of the nails is important to prevent scratches and infections. Round the fingernails and trim the toenails at right angles, in order to prevent ingrown nails (nails which pierce the skin). Then clean and file each nail.

For those confined to bed, skin care is extremely important for comfort and for the prevention of bed sores.

A good wash cleanses the skin of organic waste secreted by the sweat glands. The sebaceous glands secrete a natural oil that prevents dryness and cracking of the skin. Excessive washing can remove this oil and damage the skin.

Avoiding bed sores

When someone has been in the same reclining position for a long time, the pressure on certain parts of the body (pelvis, shoulder blades, elbows, heels and ankles) blocks the circulation of the blood to these regions. This can cause the death of cells that depend on this circulation for nourishment.

It is important at bath time to examine the person's skin for sores. Some guidelines for avoiding bed sores are the following:

– regularly change the position of the sick person in bed (every two hours, if this is possible);

– keep the person dry and clean;

– use rubbing alcohol to strengthen the skin, because alcohol coagulates the proteins of the cells—like heat coagulating the white of an egg (for elderly persons, however, it is better to use a gentle body oil since alcohol tends to dry out the skin);

– for those sick at home, recommend a water bed or the use of a lamb skin.

Care of bed sores

A gentle massage increases blood circulation. Beginning with an area that is red, move outwards, exerting a gentle pressure. The resulting increased circulation carries nourishment and oxygen to the affected region. A circular movement is most effective for increasing blood circulation.

Importance of skin care

The importance of skin care is most evident for those who are seriously sick. For them, good hygiene is not optional: it is a prerequisite for comfort.

This personal attention also gives those who are ill a deeper sense of self-worth and a more positive image of themselves. It witnesses to the respect due to every human person.

Chapter six

Proper diet

Serving meals

A therapeutic diet

A good food balance

In all that concerns food, the sick person ought to enjoy the same advantages as the healthy: nutritious food and attractive meals served with good taste and care.

A balanced diet is important for everyone, especially for those recovering from an illness. A lack of protein delays recovery and hinders the healing process. Sugars and fats provide essential energy. Vitamins, mineral salts, fibres, and, of course, water, are equally necessary components of a balanced diet.

Serving meals

The atmosphere surrounding mealtime is as important as the food itself. Attention should be given, therefore, to the preparation of the setting and to the manner in which the meals are served.

If at all possible serve the meals in a dining room rather than in the sick person's bedroom. The room can be decorated with flowers and should be well-lit (unless a more intimate atmosphere is preferred). Make the meals a social occasion—a chance to be with friends—instead of leaving the sick person to eat alone.

Careful arrangement of their trays and of the food on their plates shows respect and affection for sick persons. Present them with the menu for the day, explaining the special features of their diet. Those who are sick will eat with more enjoyment if they understand the restrictions imposed by their diet.

Before the meal

Attention to a few details will help sick persons to eat with more comfort.

– Give them an opportunity to go to the washroom themselves. If needed, assist them to visit the washroom or give them a bed pan.

– Let them wash their hands and face.

- If they must eat in bed, make them comfortable by placing pillows behind their back.

- If they are able, help them to sit in a chair and place the night table before them.

- The ideal, of course, would be to take them to an attractive dining room,

- but whatever the setting, try to create a comfortable and pleasant milieu.

During the meal

Serve the meal with a kind word. If needed, help the sick person to butter bread, to cut meat and to pour liquids.

Place a table napkin to protect their clothes; provide a paper serviette near at hand so they can wipe their hands and mouth.

If they need help eating, ask them which food they prefer to eat first. Measure out appropriate amounts for each mouthful and offer them their preferred liquids.

Throughout the meal, take care to stay within their range of vision and at their eye level.

A therapeutic diet

A therapeutic diet is a menu that is strictly regulated by a physician's instructions. This can happen, for example, in cases of obesity, of cardiac and renal illness, of high cholesterol, etc. Those who are prescribed such restrictive diets often live at home and even continue to work.

Four categories

Diets are usually classified, more or less rigorously, according to four categories.

- A full diet is a routine diet that is not really therapeutic in the strict sense of the term. It allows complete fulfillment of bodily needs according to personal tastes and preferences.

- A light diet is used for a limited time period, until the sick can return to a full diet. It allows the eating of homemade soup, Jell-O, custard, etc.

- A soft diet has a low cellulose content. It facilitates the process of feeding and digestion. All foods are strained to a purée.

– A liquid diet includes foods such as water, stock and juices. It does not produce intestinal gas and is often used after an operation.

This classification can serve as an easy reference for understanding and for more effective application of the diets prescribed by physicians for different illnesses.

A good food balance

In all cases where the physician does not prescribe a diet or specific regimen, the sick person requires food that is substantial, well-balanced and proportionate to the energy expended. It has been calculated that a person confined to bed requires a minimum of 1500 calories every day. An adult engaged in moderately strenuous work requires an average of 2400 calories a day.

Apart from vitamins and mineral salts, foods are conveniently classified in three categories corresponding to the body's specific needs: proteins, sugars and fats.

Proteins

The word "protos" means "that holds the first place." This indicates the importance of proteins for the balance of the human metabolism.

Humans and animals are not able to make their own proteins. Plants manufacture them from elements in nature (carbon, oxygen, hydrogen and nitrogen) through the process of photosynthesis. Humans and animals obtain proteins from plants, the muscles of other animals, and even from their by-products such as milk and eggs.

Proteins are contained in the following foods (the protein content of 100 grams of each food is indicated):

– meat and fish—15 to 20 grams;

– egg yokes—16 grams;

– cheese—23 to 29 grams;

– vegetables (beans, peas, etc.)—20 to 25 grams;

– almonds and walnuts—16 to 21 grams;

– flour from oats—16 grams;

– flour from wheat—12 grams.

The role of proteins is the manufacture of new tissue and the regeneration of damaged or used tissue. They balance the blood pressure and keep our immune system healthy. A defi-

ciency in proteins can cause, therefore, an arrest in growth, a lack of resistance to infections, and muscular weakness.

Sugars

Sugars provide the body with the energy necessary for life; namely, for heat and movement.

They are grouped in three categories:

– the monosaccharides (simple sugars), such as glucose or dextrose, that are found in, among other things, fruit, vegetables and honey;

– the disaccharides, such as sucrose or table sugar, that are found in sugar cane, beets and maple sap (lactose or milk sugar is also a disaccharide);

– the polysaccharides, such as starch, that are found in cereal grains, beans and dry peas, and in certain tubercular vegetables like potatoes.

Sugars and starches play an important role in the body:

– providing mechanical energy and the heat we need;

– aiding metabolism of lipides (greasy substances);

– facilitating proper functioning of the liver;

–   helping good elimination of stools by reason of their effect on the intestinal flora.

In the case of diabetes, the ingestion of certain forms of glucosides must be moderated. Fruit and vegetables, on the other hand, are nutritious sources of sugars because they are rich in mineral salts and vitamins.

Fats

Fats are greasy substances that appear in diverse forms and are necessary for bodily health. They are found in the fat of meat, vegetable oils, egg yokes, milk fat, etc.

Their principal role is the provision of calories: one gram of fat provides nine calories. In addition they insulate against the rays of the sun, the cold and even external shocks.

Fats (lipides) play an important function in the absorption of vitamin A and other vitamins that are soluble only in greasy substances. They also give flavour to foods, which helps to explain why we tend to use so much fat in our cooking.

An excess of fats leads to the formation of cholesterol in the body. Cholesterol is necessary for the proper functioning of the body, as a protective substance acting with the defence system. Too much cholesterol, however, obstructs blood circulation, contributing to hardening of the arteries.

Fats also help to cause the formation of stones in the body. They are found in great quantities in the giblets and glands of

animals: in the liver, brain, heart, egg yokes and in all animal fats, as well as in shellfish such as lobsters, oysters, etc.

The ideal diet

What is the ideal diet for the person confined to bed and able to do little exercise?

The golden rule would be to strike a balance among the three categories mentioned—proteins, sugars and fats—to the extent that the person has not been prescribed a therapeutic diet.

Apart from medical indications to the contrary, there is no restriction on salads, raw vegetables and their juices. Included in the menu should be cheese, yogurt and as much fruit as desired. There is also no restriction on cooked vegetables except for potatoes, corn, rice, and pasta that too often substitute for vegetables on our tables.

Those confined to bed will do well to add to their diet whole-wheat bread, dried prunes or prune juice, and fibre foods such as wheat or oat bran, to help the functioning of the intestines.

We are what we eat! This is doubly true for sick persons during their recovery stage. They require a well-balanced diet that gives their body what it needs to renew its strength and to regenerate itself.

Chapter seven

Moving those who are sick

Some rules for bodily movement

Walking

Using a walker

Using crutches

Using a wheelchair

Moving from a bed to a wheelchair

and from a wheelchair to a bed

Moving those who are sick can sometimes require considerable effort and care on the part of care-givers. It can also entail certain risks if the rules for bodily movement are not known and followed.

In all bodily movements such as leaning over, turning, pushing and pulling, lifting and carrying an object, it is important to apply the laws of gravity.

Some rules for bodily movement

- In order to have a firm base, separate your feet slightly, one a little in front of the other.

- Before lifting an object, distribute your weight equally on both feet.

- Correct posture: knees slightly bent, abdomen pulled in, chest raised, head straight.

By keeping your trunk aligned and straight, you protect your back muscles against tears and stress.

Execute every movement at a comfortable level. Beds are often adjustable to higher or lower positions. If you cannot adjust the bed use a stool or else crouch keeping your back straight.

Keep the object you are moving close to your body, avoiding the need to stretch yourself forward. Take care, for example, to approach the sick person from your side of the bed to give her or him a bath. When required, go around to the other side of the bed, instead of stretching across the bed and putting stress on your back.

In the same way, when carrying an object keep it close to your body. It will be lighter to carry if the line of gravity falls within your own support base. Otherwise, your leg and arm muscles must act against the force of gravity as well as support the weight of the object. If you lift a heavy object that is resting on the floor, keep your body straight and use your legs rather than your back.

In summary:

-   keep proper bodily alignment;
-   work at a comfortable level;
-   keep the object as close to your body as you can; and
-   work with your legs rather than with your back.

Walking

It is very common for sick persons to begin walking again very soon after their operation. But care is needed: relatives and volunteers ought not to move them or encourage them to move

themselves without the authorization of the physician or hospital personnel.

When you help sick persons to walk, encourage them to proceed as naturally as possible. Ask them to walk holding their body straight with the best alignment they can manage (if they are suffering pain from a recent injury). They are often afraid that their stitches or staples will tear if they hold themselves too straight. You can assure them that the mending is sufficiently strong to withstand the contractions of the muscles caused by walking.

How to physically support sick persons

If those who are sick are physically weak or lack confidence in themselves, they need your assistance to walk. It is important to know how to support them with complete safety.

When they take one step forward and are momentarily balancing on one foot, they need help to balance the weight of their body. Encourage them to walk naturally: lifting their feet, placing their heels on the floor first, shifting their weight progressively to the bottoms of their feet, and finally pushing with their toes. Have them walk in this manner instead of dragging their feet on the floor.

To support them, hold their elbow or hand with your hand. To provide a firmer support, hold their left hand with your left hand and pass your right arm around their waist. To help those who are very weak and likely to lose their balance, it is better to seek the assistance of another person.

To prevent or soften falls

Falls are the most frequent accidents in health care institutions and at home. Before attempting to walk with someone who is ill, check with the physician or personnel in charge of care to ascertain if the person has the strength and permission to walk.

Remove all objects (stools, rugs, plants, etc.) that could cause the person to fall. Avoid walking on wet surfaces.

If they become weak while they are walking, you can prevent or lighten a fall by providing as much physical support as possible. You can walk by their side, ready, if needed, to catch them by the wrists or under the armpits in order to lower them gently to the floor.

In softening their fall in this manner, take care that while leaning over you bend your knees to avoid hurting your own back.

Using a walker

A walker provides intermediate support between crutches and a wheelchair, to help sick persons to move without assistance and gradually to regain their own autonomy. Some elderly persons use light walkers because of their limited strength or in order to give them needed confidence.

For the first few practices or if you fear that they are quite weak, it is a good idea to accompany them with a seat on which they can sit in an emergency. Some walkers are even equipped with a seat for this purpose.

Using crutches

When those who are sick become stronger and more independent, encourage them to use crutches that give them greater mobility.

Crutches must be adjusted perfectly to the height and arm length of those who use them. Note that body weight is carried by the hands and never by the armpits. Some light crutches rest on the top of the arm and give even more flexibility for walking.

Stay by their side for the first few practices, especially while they are negotiating stairs or if they seem especially weak. If they find walking with crutches becomes too tiring, invite them to use the walker as a safer method.

Using a wheelchair

The wheelchair is particularly useful for ailing persons who are very weak, or for relatively long trips.

It is advisable for care-givers first to try a wheelchair themselves.

Sit in the chair, place your feet on the footrests, release the brakes and practise moving the chair by using the steering wheels. Practise steering the chair and turning it on itself.

Then ask another person to take you on an elevator, through doorways, into the cafeteria, and even along neighbouring streets. There is no better way to become aware of the fears and frustrations that ailing persons in wheelchairs experience.

Steering a wheelchair

When steering a wheelchair, exert constant pressure on the chair's two handles. To turn, exert stronger pressure with one hand.

To enter into a room with a swinging door (a washroom for example), turn the chair around completely so as to approach the door from behind. Use your body to keep the door open wide, then turn the chair again to a forward position after having let go of the door.

This method avoids injuring the arms or legs of the person in the wheelchair, and avoids making abrupt movements that could upset the person. The same procedure is used in elevators.

To go up or down stairs with a wheelchair, it is advisable to seek assistance from another person. Climb the stairs backwards, pulling up the chair without jolts, while the other person is on the stairs just below the wheelchair to give support. Descend the stairs in the same manner, with your back to the stairs.

When sick persons drive by themselves

If you notice that an ill person is able to drive the wheelchair alone, teach that person the following movements: rolling the chair, raising and lowering the footrests with their feet, putting on and releasing the breaks, and steering the chair around obstacles. If you have tried these movements yourself, you are better prepared to explain them to others.

For wheelchairs with electric motors the movements are the same, but be sure to adjust the machine to the lowest speed during the practice period, to avoid accidents.

Moving from a bed to a wheelchair and from a wheelchair to a bed

---

N.B.: Volunteers should not attempt these procedures without the permission of the physician or hospital personnel.

These procedures are most easily accomplished with two persons, but it is often necessary to do them alone. The following techniques are helpful to know in either case.

From a bed to a wheelchair

Place the wheelchair parallel to the side of the bed, with the seat turned toward the head of the bed. Put on the two breaks and pull up the footrests.

Ask the sick person, if they are able, to push their body to the edge of the bed, their legs hanging. Then have them stand up by leaning for support on your arms or shoulders.

Turn them so that their back is toward the seat of the chair. Lean over to grab hold of the arms of the chair and ask them to seat themselves slowly while leaning for support on your arms or shoulders.

When they are not able to hold themselves erect in the chair it is necessary to tie them with a belt around their waist, or to secure them around the chest.

If they are more mobile, you can follow this procedure: Position yourself facing the sick who are standing next to their bed. Support them with your left hand while holding the chair with your right hand. When they have taken their seat, help them to put their feet on the footrests.

From a wheelchair to a bed

This procedure is more difficult than the previous one, and can even require the assistance of another person.

If they have enough strength, those who are ill can raise themselves from the chair by holding onto your arms or shoul-

ders. They can then be helped to turn and to sit on the edge of the bed.

If they are unable to make these movements, ask another person for help and proceed as follows.

- Place the wheelchair by the bed, with the seat turned toward the head of the bed. Put on the breaks and raise the footrests.

- They will be reassured if you have assistance and if you show confidence yourself.

- The first care-giver places him or herself at the head and shoulders of the sick person in order to lift under the arms; the second stands at the hips and legs to lift under the hips.

- Both care-givers must slide their arms under the sick person, holding him or her as close as possible to their bodies, and, when the signal is given, lifting and placing the person on the edge of the bed.

It is important that the two care-givers synchronize their movements well so that one person does not have to carry the full weight of the ill person.

Take care, finally, that the sick person is comfortable back in bed. Adjust the pillows and covers as needed.

Chapter eight

Communicating
with a deaf person

Creating a favourable milieu

What the speaker should do

What the listener should do

Testimony: A father suffering from deafness

Hearing aids

Deafness is an invisible handicap that is often easy for us inadvertently to ignore. For those who are seriously sick this handicap is especially distressing because they easily misunderstand instructions and, consequently, risk incorrectly applying them. Moreover, this handicap can lead to a very deep sense of loneliness.

Because most persons are embarrassed by their deafness they look for ways to conceal it. They frequently have feelings of frustration and annoyance. It can be very important, therefore, for care-givers to know strategies for facilitating communication.

The following pages have been inspired by a program of hearing adjustment created by Mrs. Josette Lefrançois, audiologist at the Centre de Jour Rolland-Major, Cartierville, Quebec.

Creating a favourable milieu

Those hard of hearing have difficulty hearing when background noises drown out the articulation of consonants. This is particularly true of those who wear a hearing aid.

For a long and important conversation, therefore, it helps to lower the volume of the radio or television and to turn off noisy fans or air conditioners.

Try to avoid making unnecessary noises, for example with utensils you use during meals. If possible don't hold an important conversation in a busy and distracting place or outdoors when a high wind is blowing.

What the speaker should do

Here are five golden rules for a good conversation with someone who is hard of hearing.

First rule: position yourself in front of those you are speaking to, at a maximum distance of three metres, in full light. It is important that they can follow the movement of your lips. Do not move your head too much and avoid speaking with your hand before your mouth, while chewing, or with a cigarette between your lips!

Second rule: help your listeners to understand quickly what you are saying. Attract their attention before beginning to speak and give them an idea of what subject is to be addressed. Be as familiar as you can be with their situation and their manner of naming persons and places. Give them important information in writing: the names of persons, addresses, telephone numbers, etc.

Third rule: speak in short and simple sentences, avoiding long, complicated phrases, puns, jumping from subject to subject. If they have not well understood what has been said, do not simply repeat the same phrase but say it in other words.

Fourth rule: speak a little louder than usual but without shouting. Most frequently the consonants are poorly understood, especially the "hidden" consonants such as C, D, G, L, R and S. Speak at a normal speed, articulating the consonants well.

Fifth rule: emphasize the conversation with natural gestures, without exaggeration. Direct attention to your face rather than to your hands.

In group situations, position deaf persons so that they can see everyone present. For small meetings, sit in a circle if this is possible. And don't all speak at once!

In formal groups, the facilitator ought to summarize what people have just expressed, underlining changes in the subject of conversation. The facilitator should also encourage sharing in small groups where participation is better.

What the listener should do

Those who are hard of hearing do well to devise their own listening strategies that will help them to function in society.

They should openly inform those with whom they are speaking of their hearing difficulties, asking them to speak more slowly or louder as is needed.

In order to see the movement of others' lips, they can sit with their backs to the light, asking others to position themselves in clear view.

When they have not clearly understood what has been said, they should not hesitate to ask that it be repeated, especially if

the subject of conversation seems to be important. Sometimes the instructions of physicians and hospital personnel are misunderstood, and therefore there is a risk these instructions will be incorrectly applied.

In groups, those who are hard of hearing shouldn't hesitate to ask someone to clarify the subject of conversation, to repeat important statements and to summarize a confusing discussion. Often these questions will also benefit other people in the group who seem to understand what is going on, but really don't!

Testimony:
A father suffering from deafness

(Testimony of his daughter)

My father suffers from a buzzing in the ears that is more or less intense, causing total deafness of the left ear and partial deafness of the right ear. I must confess that sometimes I am at a loss to know how to help him.

Because he is very proud, my father does not easily admit that he is handicapped. He has developed several strategies for not letting his deafness show in order to lessen his suffering. He chooses to speak a great deal, for example, rather than let himself be put in a listening posture, although this is not always possible.

At one family get-together of nine persons, where everyone was speaking rapidly and almost all at the same time, I became aware that he had understood nothing. He acted as if nothing was wrong, but I could tell by the distant look on his face that he had withdrawn.

I spoke to him to confirm my observations, and he responded with both surprise and pleasure: "How can you know that I have not understood?" I told him that by his serious, steady gaze I could see that he was not really following the conversation.

I have developed a skill in reading people's expressions through teaching a second language: a person who does not understand a language often has the same reactions as someone who is deaf and develops similar coping strategies.

These few, simple words of explanation allowed him to re-enter the group—that is to say, to remain with us—and showed me it is through small details that we are connected to life.

B.L.

There are different types of hearing aids for amplifying sound: they can be worn in one's ear or concealed in the arm of one's glasses.

The volume ought to be adjusted carefully, neither too weak nor too loud. Usually the toothed wheel is to be turned to two-thirds of top volume, never to maximum.

It takes a good deal of practice to learn how to use such an aid to full advantage. It is advisable to use it first for intimate conversations, since in groups the confusing and poorly directed sound does not facilitate good hearing.

Cleaning the hearing aid

The hearing tip should always be clean and free of ear wax. If dirt accumulates in the opening, the sound cannot reach the ear. It should be cleaned with toothpicks.

Take off the tip and wash it in water and gentle soap. Never use alcohol since this could dry out and crack the plastic.

Checking the battery

All hearing aids operate with batteries, some of them rechargeable. If the battery is too weak the sound will be distorted and the hearing less clear. The battery can be checked using an inexpensive voltmeter. And the life of the battery can be lengthened by turning off the aid when it is not being used for an extended period of time.

Those who give care to elderly persons will find that hearing problems are common among them. In addition to following the suggestions mentioned above, these care-givers will do well to ask tactfully if the elderly person has understood what has been said. This applies especially when the subject matter is important.

For people with hearing problems who are ill, write down the most important words such as the name of the medication, the times for taking it, appointments with the physician, etc.

Chapter nine

Assisting those who are visually handicapped

Our attitude toward blind persons

How to guide a blind person

Meals for those who are blind

Testimony: My visually handicapped mother

I t is difficult to act naturally with someone who is blind because of the strong impact this handicap has on us and the feeling of helplessness it leaves with us.

The challenges of blindness

For those who are blind, each day offers challenges to be overcome. The thousand and one details of life are so many problems, sometimes complex, that must be resolved one by one.

For those who have had sight, blindness is an anguishing trial. The adjustment to their new situation can be long and hard if they cut themselves off from others and try to rely solely on themselves. If, on the other hand, they accept living with their handicap and seek help from others, they are able to find work and to live in many ways a normal existence.

Our attitude toward blind persons

We have a tendency, too often, to treat blind people as if they are children, not acknowledging that they are adult, autonomous persons capable of making their own decisions and directing their own lives.

We sometimes speak loudly to them as if they are hard of hearing. Or we try to do everything for them as if they aren't able to do things for themselves. On the contrary, we should be encouraging them to use to the fullest the capacities and skills they have.

When you see a blind man travelling alone, for example, you need not automatically conclude that he needs help. Ask him directly and simply. If he accepts, offer him your arm or respond to his need.

In your contacts with blind people try to be as natural as possible in your way of speaking and manner of acting. In particular, it helps to tell them what you see, to describe the scenery and colours. Remember that your gestures are not helpful for communication.

At the initial contact identify yourself by your name and shake their hand or give them a kiss, depending on whatever is appropriate. Your voice and this physical contact will be for the blind person an important sign of warmth, of friendship and of acceptance.

How to guide a blind person

Extend your arm simply to them. They will grasp your elbow and follow you, a step behind. The movements of your body will warn them if there are stairs to climb or descend, or if there is an obstacle to walk around. Remember to watch out so they don't bang their heads or bump into other objects.

Those who are blind can manage very well in rooms with which they are familiar, as long as no one has moved furniture around without telling them. It helps to leave signs to give them directions: tape on doors, boxes of different shapes, etc.

When you enter a room with the visually handicapped, describe the room with the people and objects found there. Take them to the people present and introduce them to those you know. When you invite blind people to dinner or accompany them out to a meal, describe to them what is on the table and on their plate so that they don't accidentally knock over something. If they drop food on their clothing, tell them at once so that they can immediately remove it.

Meals can be moments of irritation and frustration for blind people if care has not been taken in advance to make proper arrangements.

Always place eating utensils in the same order around their plate so that they can easily find them. The same applies to other objects on the table or tray.

The hands of a dial are sometimes used to help blind persons to know how their food is arranged on their plate or tray: "The meat is at nine o'clock, the peas at midnight, the potatoes at three o'clock."

Tactfully offer them the help they need, cutting their meat, for example, or pouring their liquids.

For a full and complete life

Blind people have a wonderful capacity for growth and for contributing to the life of their milieu. The role of care-givers can be to encourage them to be open to the external world, through listening to the radio, reading in Braille, and joining in activities—social and otherwise—that help them to grow.

Blind people bring extraordinary life, courage and good humour to others.

Testimony:
My visually handicapped mother

(Testimony of her daughter)

(The mother of eight children, Angelina became blind at the age of 72 and lost her husband shortly afterwards. She lives now with her eldest daughter who helps her in simple ways and marvels at her courage and determination.)

Angelina is a woman of faith and determination admired by all who know her.

She decided that she would stay in her own place if a homemaker could visit her to prepare her noon and evening meals. My sister and I would share the remaining tasks. "My good guardian angel will take care of everything," she assured us. As it turned out, a neighbour living on the same street agreed to come, Monday to Friday, two hours in the morning and two hours in the afternoon. She prepared the meals following menus chosen by Angelina, did the daily cleaning, accompanied her on her health walks, perused her mail, and read to her, which she loved.

Angelina was thus the mistress in her own home. And the hours and days of her life passed without her complaining of boredom: "My prayers and my radio programs take up all my time; then there is my correspondence to do every day." Angelina actually kept up a correspondence with several people. She taped letters into a machine. "I was a shorthand typist when I was young," she confided.

Fridays, Saturdays and Sundays, Angelina was completely alone. She ate salads and soups prepared in advance by Madame Pépin. She knew her kitchen by heart and knew how to regulate the stove. When we went to visit her, she made sure before we took our vacation that the stove and lights were turned off, the chairs were in their place, the litre of milk and litre of juice were in the refrigerator....

One day last year, Madame Pépin called me with a worried tone in her voice: "Your mother does not want me to tell you, but she fainted, and today it has me frightened...." That very day I decided that my mother would not move to a residence, unless it was mine.

Angelina moved, therefore, to my home. I had been a widow for two years and had only a son to take care of. I offered her the biggest room with a window opening onto the garden so that she could hear the birds singing and smell the fresh perfume from the lilacs and apple trees in the spring.

Hardly a week later Angelina was comfortably settled in her new residence. She always ate her breakfast alone. The essentials were kept in a cupboard reserved for her.

She also had her own space in the refrigerator and bathroom and knew where to find her things. I prepared vegetarian meals for her with a special chicken dinner from time to time. Periodically I prepared a bubble bath for her and gave her a herbal shampoo for her long silver hair. I also cut her hair "in the waning of the moon, because under its influence the hair is restored," she used to say.

When I had to leave for my errands, I placed the telephone near her chair. She had memorized and knew how to dial the numbers of each of her children, her friends, and the neighbour who lived above. Since she loved to hear her radio programs, she wore headphones to respect my need for quiet.

When the children and grandchildren came to visit they always knocked at grandmother's door and brought her a little treat or offered to read to her. In exchange she shared with them her roaring laughter and a hug—accompanied by "Oh! How you have grown!"—and, of course, her deep gratitude for the least sign of attention.

At different hours of the day, during the week and on Sundays when the Mass was celebrated on television, behind the closed door of Angelina's kingdom, I heard her humming songs of love and hymns to the Lord.... Then my soul trembled with emotion and my eyes became misty.

Her eldest daughter, Aline.

Chapter ten

The art
of being with someone
who is lonely

The importance of good communication

Verbal and non-verbal communication

Four attitudes conducive to good communication

Obstacles to effective communication

At different stages of their illness, many of those who are sick go through periods of withdrawal and deep depression. They are fortunate if, during these painful moments, they are visited by someone with an attentive ear and a loving heart: someone who can share their anxieties, pain, hopes and fears.

Emotional suffering and physical pain are intimately related. This means that if those who are ill are able to verbalize the emotions they are feeling about their past history or about what they are presently experiencing, they can find relief from some of their physical pain. That is one reason why different people who are sick with the same illnesses do not necessarily experience the same intensity of pain.

The loneliness suffered by those who are immobilized by illness often has its source in their lack of contact and communication with persons from their familiar surroundings. When this has been lacking, the first step is to re-establish such meaningful contact.

Communication is first of all the art of listening to and understanding the messages of others, who are sharing what they feel, think or believe. It also means sharing, in turn, who you are, what you are thinking and what you believe.

All genuine communication is based on the fundamental attitudes of respect and love, both for yourself and for those persons with whom you are sharing.

Verbal and non-verbal communication

In a good conversation each person plays, one after the other, the roles of transmitter and receiver.

The transmitter is the person who is sending a message. A sick person might say hello, for example, expressing his or her happiness in seeing you again.

The receiver is the person who receives the message. When you hear the person telling you of her or his joy in seeing you, you pick up the invitation to enter into a personal relationship.

In such communication the non-verbal signs are four times more effective than the verbal signs. The facial expression, the body's posture, the hands and eyes communicate at a deeper level than even the spoken word. It is the whole body with all of its movements that expresses one's being.

These signs reveal the person, who one is, what one feels, the real self. If we take the example of two persons who are in love, a single glance is all that is needed for them to deeply understand each other.

If those you are visiting are frustrated and angry, you will quickly know their true feelings by observing their eyes and gestures. How will you deal with these feelings? Will you be able to accept these persons with all that they are living in the present moment?

Four attitudes conducive to good communication

In order to establish good communication, it is necessary to develop four fundamental attitudes: confidence in others, empathy, acceptance of self and of others, and authenticity.

Having confidence in and accepting others

If you have confidence in those you are visiting, you will allow them to be completely themselves, even if that makes you feel uncomfortable. You will let them share whatever they wish, by assuming an attitude of "unconditional acceptance." And you will be capable of being yourself with them.

In practice, the better you know the people you are visiting the more naturally you will accept them and have confidence in them. Attention to the psychological traits of each sick person, as briefly outlined in Chapter Two, can help to deepen your personal experience and understanding of those you visit.

Being empathic and accepting one's self

An attitude of empathy allows you, through your own feelings, to be sensitive to the feelings of others: to go beyond their words in order to enter into their world, to sense how they are feeling interiorly.

How do the sick you are visiting envisage what is now happening to them? What do they feel toward you? What is their attitude to life?

You will never be able to understand and accept the sick person unless you have learned to accept yourself.

Painful experiences such as sickness can lead you to be more truly yourself. How many people have made great changes in their lives and experienced a heightened self-awareness after having lived through personal losses? These experiences can have a maturing effect and help you to live in greater empathy with the sick.

Being authentic

To be authentic is to live truth in your lives—that is, to have congruence between who you are and what you say or do. Authenticity flows from a high level of self-knowledge and self-acceptance. It requires interior stability and a balanced personality. And as a state of integrity that insures reliability and trust, authenticity is a prerequisite for good communication with the sick.

Being authentic includes the following traits:

- a high degree of honesty: you do not pretend to have feelings that you do not have;

- a comprehensive view of the human personality: you consider all the levels of the personality to be important—the physical, psychological, mental and spiritual;

- an acceptance of the distinctive character of each person: you respect each one's own mystery and unique path;

- an ability to act intuitively: you are not a slave to abstract theories or to the authority of others.

Obstacles to effective communication

Serious obstacles to effective communication can arise from limitations or blocks in one's fundamental attitudes. Hypocrisy is such an attitude, the roots of which can often be traced to the education one has received.

A simple but common example of hypocrisy would be telling sick people that they are looking better, in order to please them, even though you know that it is not true. Another example is when you pretend that you are feeling well (or ill) when the opposite is the case. What you are doing, in effect, is refusing to share your real feelings, and this closed attitude creates an obstacle to good communication.

There can be many reasons for such hypocritical behaviour: difficulty knowing your real feelings; an excessive need to be liked, so you say what you think the other person wants to hear; lack of respect for their right and strength to handle the truth of their own condition, so you treat them like children by trying to overprotect them; projection of your own fears onto the sick person, if you have difficulty dealing with pain or other feelings in your own life. Underlying all of these reasons, however, is essentially a lack of self-love and self-acceptance on the part of the visitor.

Bodily postures can also reflect interior attitudes that are obstacles to communication. Certain positions can reveal an attitude of resistance or exclusion. Sitting with arms and legs tightly crossed, for example, can show a lack of openness to the other. This attitude goes along with tension in the neck that also contributes to blocking communication.

Those visitors who have built around themselves such protective walls should leave to others the privilege of entering into a personal relationship with sick persons, until they feel themselves ready for such intimate communication.

Part three

Ministering to those who are sick

Chapter eleven

The visiting care-giver and active listening

Available for listening

Available for loving

Those suffering from illness often feel disoriented. If they are hospitalized, their lives are regulated by endless medical procedures, their days divided up by a succession of short, unscheduled visits by countless specialists. One patient counted up to thirty-two different persons who crossed the threshold of her door in a single day, and most of them did not identify themselves. If they are at home, sick persons can easily become fatigued by the monotonous routine.

In order to keep a sense of peace and equilibrium, both in the hospital and at home, these people need someone who can bring a warmth that comforts, a presence that relieves their suffering, a smile that calms and gives hope.

What satisfaction to find an attentive ear, ready to listen! A principal role of the visiting care-giver is to bring, through his or her active listening, the comfort that they seek.

Very few people in our world, closed in as it is on itself and so pressed for time, know how to truly listen or take the time to do so.

Sick people, however, are not numbers. They preserve their secret selves and need to be acknowledged for who they are, unique persons living through some difficult moments. They will always be gratified to meet someone who is available to listen and to accompany them for a few moments.

The qualities of listening

What does it really mean "to listen" to someone?

–   To listen is to offer a place in our hearts, to accept to be the mirror of another person. Through relating with another person, those who are sick understand better what is weighing on their hearts: they know themselves better. This warm presence helps to soothe their fears, their loneliness and depression.

–   To listen is to welcome another by creating a vacuum within ourselves, and to invite the other to occupy that void. This openness implies an attitude of simplicity and spontaneity: by concentrating our interest on those who are sick, we create an atmosphere of trust. They feel themselves to be known, not judged, and can freely speak of what is upsetting them.

–   To listen is to be one's self with the other, in truth and authenticity. Authenticity is the correspondence between what the care-giver feels or thinks and what he or she communicates to the sick person. Authentic persons let go of their masks and feel free to be themselves with others.

–   To listen is to have a positive attitude toward one's self and toward others. The simple fact of listening possesses a surprising healing power. And the word is often a more effective remedy than many medications.

When I ask you to listen to me...

When I ask you to listen to me
and you start giving advice,
you have not done what I asked.

When I ask you to listen to me
and you begin to tell me why I shouldn't feel that way,
you are trampling on my feelings.

When I ask you to listen to me
and you feel you have to do something to solve my problems,
you have failed me, strange as that may seem.

Perhaps that's why prayer works for some people.
Because God is mute
and doesn't offer advice or try to fix things.
God just listens and trusts you to work it out for yourself.

So please, just listen and hear me.
And if you want to talk,
wait a few minutes for your turn
and I promise I'll listen to you.

(Anonymous poem cited by Leo Buscaglia
in *Loving Each Other*, pp. 67-68)

Good humour

One of the greatest difficulties of active listening, especially when the ill person is depressed or aggressive, is to preserve a sense of good humour throughout the visit. Human communication is made up of signs and very subtle messages. People who are sick are ultra-sensitive and quickly perceive our feelings and reactions. If they see before them a person with a negative attitude, they will want nothing more than to cut short the visit. If, on the other hand, they find they are with a person who has a positive attitude, they will take comfort in this difficult time of their illness.

– To listen, finally, is to assure the other of our discretion. Those afflicted by illness expect discretion not only from their physicians and health-care workers but also from the visitors with whom they share their confidences.

A person suffering from cancer or AIDS will not want her or his sickness talked about by all who come by. The discretion asked of the visiting care-givers is of the same standard as that required of health-care professionals.

Listening

These hours of union at the deepest level of our two beings, these hours of mutual listening are always too short. I would want to stretch out these privileged moments.

The friendship that I have lived and I live even now calls me to an ever greater listening. For it is in listening that I learn to know you better, to understand you better, to love you better.

Can I tell you that my heart understands what you do not say?...Can I tell you that your silence is eloquent?...

Your silence hides nothing....It is revealing; it has an unbelievable transparency. It lets through, without filtering, your simplicity, your honesty, your purity, your goodness and your noble-mindedness. I can only marvel before you.

You possess an extraordinary power and my only regret is to note that many times you do not see yourself as you really are. Your mirror does not do you justice....In observing yourself you see only your weaknesses. Tell me, when will you see yourself as you really are?

I love to be with you. I love the moments that we spend together disclosing ourselves as we share our secrets. But I especially love our moments of silence. For it is in these moments that listening is easiest for me.

(Unedited poem by Émile Émond)

When we visit those who are ill we accept to share with them a little of our time. It is good to tell them how much time we have available, so that they will not be disappointed when we have to leave.

These few minutes will then be entirely devoted to the other, with a presence of the heart: "The quality of our listening depends on the quality of our heart and not on our hearing capacity" (Françoise Durkenne, *Le Temp de la bienveillance*). In order to understand another person in depth, does it not require a quality of presence that is virtually beyond measure?

An authentic love

When we visit people who are ill, we assume the role of a life-giving sun. Through our contacts we enliven them to deepen their faith and hope, their taste for life, or at least their acceptance of a fatal illness.

Our action is motivated by "gift love" and not by "possessive love." This is an attitude found among those whose love is authentic. Such a love is the fruit of inner harmony; it fosters interaction between two beings, like a magic energy that achieves miracles.

The evangelist Luke narrates that one day Jesus was standing in the middle of a crowd that was pressing him from all sides. "A woman suffering from an incurable hemorrhage for twelve years came up behind Jesus and touched the fringe of his cloak. The hemorrhage stopped immediately. Jesus said, 'Who touched me?' When they all denied that they had, Peter and his companions said, 'Master, it is the crowds around you, pushing.' But Jesus said, 'Somebody touched me. I felt power going out from me'" (Luke 8:43-46).

Later Jesus will say to his disciples: "Whatever I do you can do, and even more." We enjoy surprising powers of healing, therefore, if we are truly present to sick persons with an authentic love.

A double happiness

Visiting those who are sick is a source of happiness for two persons: for the one who receives and for the one who gives. Is not our role as volunteers to bring happiness to those whom we visit?

But by a strange paradox the happiness of the one who gives is, without any doubt, still greater. "*As long as you live in love, no one can take away your joy. Joy is the inner expansion of the*

Love who has come. Love and joy give birth to peace" (Peter Deunov, *L'amour universel*).

To wish to give joy to those whom we visit: that is true love. And the persons visited, no matter how overwhelmed, will receive from us the most beautiful of gifts: our joy in living. Their path of suffering might become, through our intervention, a path toward the fullness of love.

Chapter twelve

The visiting care-giver and those suffering from specific illnesses

Those who are chronically ill

Those who are confused

The person with AIDS

The needs of people who are sick vary greatly depending on the state of their illness and the manner in which they are living through its various stages, from the initial discomfort, to the loss of autonomy, to the terminal stage.

Visitors should make an effort, therefore, to inform themselves well about the actual state of those they are visiting, so that they can respond most effectively to their changing needs.

Whatever the situation might be, the first objective of the care-giver is to insure the person's quality of life, physically, mentally and spiritually. Equally important as the sick person's need for relief from pain and suffering is the support they require to find a meaning for their lives and to better accept the progressive deterioration of their health.

At every stage of their journey, they will want respect and friendship from those who care for them. They may also yearn for transcendence, namely, to believe that they are called to something more, to meaningful directions guided by God's providence.

Those who are chronically ill

Certain illnesses progress very slowly and can continue for many years. Those who have these illnesses are considered to be chronically ill. Whether they live in the hospital or at home, those who are chronically ill have specific needs and frustrations that visiting care-givers can seek to alleviate. Those who are hospitalized risk being treated like numbers, due to the rules, routines and structures so common in complex organizations. These sick people remain persons, however, with their own identities and particular ways of viewing life. If they are to survive, they must develop ways of adapting to this new milieu.

Beatitudes of an elderly man

Happy are those who show an understanding for my feet
that stumble and for my hand that trembles!
Happy are those who understand
that my ear must strain
to grasp all that is said to me!
Happy are those who seem to know that my eyes are
glazed and my thoughts slow!
Happy are those who stay with me their faces beaming
to have a chat with me!
Happy are those who never say:
"That story, you've already told me twice today!"
Happy are those who know how to rekindle in me
memories of the past!
Happy are those who let me feel that I am loved,
valued, and not left to myself!
Happy are those who in their goodness help me
to live my last days on the road
of the eternal homeland!

Author unknown

Visiting care-givers can help them greatly, during this phase of adaptation, to recognize their right to be listened to, to be respected and accepted for who they are, with their own strengths and limitations.

Visitors can especially seek to assure that sick people experience, with the members of their families, their right to love and to be loved, to feel themselves useful despite their illness. On this last point, care-givers might encourage those they visit to contribute to the life of the institution in ways that could demonstrate their usefulness and deepen their sense of meaning.

The chronically ill require an inspiring and stimulating environment. Care-givers do well to familiarize themselves with their tastes and interests. A sterile and boring milieu encourages passive behaviour and resignation, while a stimulating environment encourages activity and a sense of responsibility.

Rather than relying on these theoretical statements, let us read the living testimony of a woman who was hospitalized for many years.

The grouchy old woman

What do you see, you who come to care,
what do you see?
What are you thinking, when you look at me?
A grouchy old woman, a bit of a fool,
an empty stare, that is no longer quite there,
who dribbles her food and does not reply;
and when you say in a loud voice "try,"
seems not to notice what you do
and always is losing her stocking and shoe,
who, docile or not, lets you do as you may
the bath and the meals to pass the long grey day.

Is that what you think, is that what you see?
Then open your eyes, that is not me.
I'll tell you who I am, as I sit here so still,
disturbing me with your rules,
eating when you will.

I'm the youngest of ten, with a father and mother,
with brothers and sisters who love one another.
A young girl of sixteen, with wings on her feet,
dreaming that soon a fiancé she'll meet.
Married at twenty, my heart jumping for joy
remembering the vows I made on that day.

I'm twenty-five now and a child at my breast
who needs a new home for his head to rest.
A woman of thirty, my child grows so fast,
we are bound to each other by ties that will last.
Forty years, and soon he'll no longer be here,

but my husband still watches over me near.
Fifty years, again babies play at my knee;
we are once more with children,
my loved-one and me.

Now the black days arrive, my husband is dead.
I look to the future with fear and dread
for my children are busy bringing up their own
and I think of past years
and the love I have known.

I have become old now and nature is cruel
amusing itself treating old age like a fool.
My body decays, grace and energy gone.
And now there's a stone where once was a heart
but in this old frame the young girl lives on.
The old heart still beats with hardly a break.

I remember the joys, I remember the pain
I revisit my life and love all over again.
I rethink past years, too short, too quickly past,
and accept the harsh fact that nothing can last.

So open your eyes, you who care for me,
and look...
not a grouchy old woman,
look closer, you will see.

(Poem found among the papers
of an old woman who died in the hospital.)

When we speak of persons who are confused, we refer to many different conditions.

Different levels of confusion

Some of those who are sick become temporarily confused, for example, following an anaesthesia, because of too strong a medication, or due to an infectious or vascular disease, etc. This acute confusion, also called delirium, is sometimes reversible if the cause itself is reversible and the brain damage minimal.

Global deterioration of the intellectual functions affecting the capacity to know—without changing consciousness, and lasting longer than three months—is called dementia. Certain types of dementia are sometimes reversible. Degenerative dementia, called Alzheimer disease, is, unfortunately, not reversible.

Elderly people also sometimes experience periods of confusion called "loss of benign memory," consisting of memory loss

and some awkwardness. The degeneration is gradual and does not, generally, greatly affect their judgment or manner of living.

A person's confusion can be aggravated by particular circumstances: partial deafness, weakening of the eyesight, loss of memory, etc.

Another very important factor is the local environment to which elderly sick persons have grown accustomed. When they are used to always living according to the same routine, in the same residence or neighbourhood, and receive little outside information, their sense of time and space can easily become disoriented when changes take place. For this reason it is important to give elderly people regular information about all aspects of their lives.

The causes and effects of confusion

A sick person can become confused for different reasons such as: a fever, an overdose or withdrawal of medications, a cerebral vascular accident, poisoning, a blow on the head, a brain tumor or a progressive degeneration of the nervous system.

Mental confusion manifests itself in different ways, depending on the individuals involved and the circumstances. There will be, for example:

–   a greater irritability shown through gestures or through impatient words and angry responses to events that are of little importance;

–   a withdrawal from social groups with whom the person lives; the person becomes suspicious and withdrawn;

–   a lack of energy; the person becomes passive, does not co-operate or contribute to personal care or respond to attention offered; in the extreme, there can be urinary and fecal incontinence;

–   a general regression that leads often to severe depression.

Responding to the needs of those who are confused

In order to really help those who are confused, the visiting care-givers must have confidence in the therapeutic value of their presence with them. The following attitudes and gestures can be helpful:

–   create around them an atmosphere that is peaceful and happy, organizing a regular routine with which those who are sick can feel comfortable;

– speak clearly and simply, in a language suitable for an adult; respond to their questions carefully, regularly informing them about the day of the week, special events, etc.;

– call them by their accustomed names (do not use their first names unless they want you to);

– confused persons are often more familiar with the past than with the present; it is good to have them talk about their past so that they can express these memories.

Although it is true that the visits of volunteers or relatives cannot remove all of the conflicts and frustrations felt by those suffering from confusion, they are a positive factor helping them to cling to reality and to their identity.

Alzheimer disease

We must mention the illness that strikes millions of people and causes so much anguish among the members of their families.

In the first stages of Alzheimer disease, those who are sick have memory losses and lose contact with reality. Their diminished awareness of what is happening provokes feelings of insecurity and anxiety. As the sickness worsens, the suffering increases. They feel vulnerable, their mental world shrinks and they are overwhelmed by a sense of powerlessness in the face of all of these losses.

They can then become very nervous and agitated, sometimes having fits of anger they never had before, and often over nothing. All of these symptoms indicate that the illness is progressively getting worse. In a more advanced stage they return to a state of calmness and indifference, since their memory loss prevents them from being aware of the seriousness of their condition.

Faced with this deterioration, the family and friends do not know what behaviour to adopt. In this situation, both loved-ones and volunteers must learn to accept the painful reality and seek to bring to the confused person all the love and tenderness that they can give.

My mother suffers
from Alzheimer disease

(Testimony of her daughter)

In a text written by Marc Oraison, the statement that has struck me the most is the following:

"When a relationship is successful, satisfying, growing, each one has the impression of being more oneself thanks to the relationship with the other: the proper distance, perhaps physical, in any case psychological and affective, has been found."

I have often experienced something similar during my last four years in palliative care. When the situation is painful and a threat to my emotional-psychological balance, I must adjust the button "focus" in order to re-establish the proper distance. But I find this difficult to do with my mother who is suffering from Alzheimer disease.

Following a bout of fatigue at the beginning of May, I consulted my family physician who strongly suggested that I not visit my mother during the several weeks I needed to recuperate. He told me that I must establish a "geographic" distance first if I wanted to have a satisfying relationship with her that would not rob me of my objectivity and energy.

I was feeling very unhappy, frustrated, angry, guilty, and especially powerless since she had begun to deteriorate mentally. These feelings heightened, principally since I had her moved to a residence. I sensed that this situation was confronting me with my own limitations and frailty. What a shock!

I was saddened to abandon my mother in the state she was in. I did not want nor could I allow to disappear the relationship that we had had for thirty-five years. However, the relationship that we have today is unsatisfying since it makes me so unhappy. What should I do? Since my mother can do nothing to change the situation it is up to me to find a solution. It is my psychological and emotional distance that must change. I must look at my mother with different eyes. I am not the one responsible for this damn disease.

My mother suffers less than I psychologically since she is more or less aware of the changes taking place in her as the disease worsens. Physically she feels very well.

She will never return to what she was before, no matter what I do. She does not remember my last visit to the residence. She seems happy to see me but does not seem to notice whether I stay one hour or three.

She is safe and is well cared for. She is lively and I can still relate with her at a different level. She still loves to laugh, to dance, to touch, to give and receive signs of affection.

She is alive. All that she has given to me remains. She is still my mother, my only mother, the same one, only sick. I must adjust to the situation so that our relationship does not end but becomes more positive.

"Despite the narrowing of hope and of plans," again writes Marc Oraison, "we cannot say that there has been a narrowing of our hope, of our will to be."

D.L.

The person with AIDS

AIDS is a worldwide epidemic. The World Health Organization in September, 1990, estimated that there are 278,038 cases of AIDS worldwide. The Organization has also estimated that by 1991 from 500,000 to 3 million people will be afflicted with this dreaded disease.

In Canada there are 4,427 cases, of whom 2,518 have died as of September 4, 1990. Because these figures are rapidly growing, soon virtually all of us will know someone who is dying of this disease.

The person who has AIDS

Persons who have AIDS have a virus for which there is no known cure. They are often rejected by family, friends, and by society in general, due to the many prejudices that this disease provokes.

Like anyone suffering from a terminal illness, persons who have AIDS need to speak about their pain and sorrow. They require the best of physical care, but they especially need accompaniment and compassionate support to be able to live to the fullest the last stages of their lives.

They ask to be understood and not to be judged, to be accepted for who they are in their uniqueness as persons. Caregivers who want to reach out to persons with AIDS must be aware of the distinctive characteristics of this disease, with the social prejudices that often surround it. They must also have faced their own personal biases related to AIDS.

What is AIDS?

AIDS (Acquired Immunodeficiency Syndrome) is caused by a virus that attacks the body's immune system. Those who have the disease no longer have the capacity to defend themselves against other viruses and microbes, and thus become vulnerable to all sorts of infections and cancers. This virus, commonly called the Human Immunodeficiency Virus (HIV), enters the bloodstream and kills the white blood cells called helper-T cells that are needed to fight disease.

Infection with this virus does not always lead to AIDS, but with time an increasing number of people who are infected develop AIDS.

What are the symptoms of the AIDS virus?

It is important to understand that some of the symptoms of the AIDS virus resemble the symptoms of other diseases. Many of them may be simply symptoms of stress. The most common symptoms are the following:

- unexplained, persistent fatigue;

- unexplained fever, shaking chills or drenching night sweats;

- unexplained weight loss;

- swollen glands (enlarged lymph nodes usually in the neck, armpits or groin) that are otherwise unexplained;

- persistent diarrhea;

- unexplained bleeding from any body opening;

- rose-violet marks appearing under the skin, in the mouth, the nose, the eyelids;

- persistent white spots known as "thrush" in the mouth;

- persistent dry cough;

- headaches, weakness or numbness in the arms or legs.

Some of these symptoms may occur only as the virus infection worsens. In combination these symptoms are called AIDS-Related Complex (ARC). The most advanced and fatal stage of the infection is defined as AIDS, when the damage to the immune system is so severe that other life-threatening opportunistic infections, cancers or brain disease occur. Pneumocystis carinii pneumonia and Kaposi's sarcoma are two of the most common diseases.

How is AIDS transmitted?

The AIDS virus is found primarily in the blood, semen or vaginal fluid of an infected person and is transmitted when any one of these enters into another person's bloodstream. This can happen through the following circumstances: sexual contact; contaminated needles or syringes used for drug injections; from an infected mother to her baby by breast-feeding; the transfusion of infected blood or blood products; and accidents with infected blood in hospitals and laboratories.

AIDS is not easy to catch. It is transmitted only by specific risk behaviours. It is not nearly as contagious, for example, as the flu, colds, measles, and other more common illnesses. And there is no evidence that it can be contacted through air, water, food, or casual body contact. There are no cases of the transmission of AIDS due to contact with tears or saliva.

Precautions to be taken when with a person who has AIDS

AIDS will not be caught from a handshake or a hug, or from objects touched, clothes worn or eating utensils used by the person who has AIDS.

If it is necessary to handle bodily fluids such as blood, semen, feces and urine of AIDS patients, it is important to follow good hygiene and normal infection control practices.

Protective clothing, such as masks and gloves, is sometimes needed to protect the patient from germs the visitor might carry. Those wearing such clothing should carefully explain to the patient the reasons for such precautions.

How to help those who have AIDS

Persons who have AIDS often continue to live for many years after they have contracted the disease. But their health deteriorates, sometimes suddenly and dramatically, at other times very gradually. As this deterioration progresses the AIDS patient needs more support and companionship. In order to be capable of providing this suppport, visiting care-givers must first of all overcome any fears or prejudices they might have about this illness.

Some have wrongly identified AIDS as a homosexual disease and have inflicted on the sick person their own fears of sexuality. Others have incorrectly viewed AIDS as God's punishment against those who have the disease. And there are those whose fear of catching the disease has led them to treat AIDS patients impersonally and without respect. Anyone with attitudes such as these cannot really support those who have AIDS.

Two ordeals bring distress to people with AIDS: fear of the unknown and the feeling of isolation. They do not wish to be treated as social outcasts or thought of as victims. Our accompaniment ought to help them to maintain hope, to think positively, to make the most of the time they have left to live.

Visiting care-givers help by being understanding, avoiding judgmental attitudes and listening attentively. They can enter into the emotional world of those who are sick, enabling them to express their fears and hopes, and supporting them as they struggle to understand the meaning of this illness for their lives.

The families and friends of persons with AIDS are often very ill-prepared to deal with the impact of this disease. Their confusion can lead them even to reject their sick relative or friend and thus to further aggravate the situation. They too need someone with whom they can confide, someone who will

The testimony of a care-giver talking to a person with AIDS

(Elizabeth Kübler-Ross narrates in her book entitled AIDS [1987, pp. 247-248] the dialogue and attitudes of Irene when she is talking to Peter who is seriously sick with AIDS.)

One morning I was sitting by my phone when it rang. I picked it up and the voice on the other end said:

"Good morning, Irene, this is Peter."

"Good morning, Peter."

"Irene, I'm dying."

"Yes, Peter, what can I do for you?"

"Irene, do you know the stage in dying when all of a sudden your psyche opens out in front of you and all of your unfinished business is right there, just like an old movie going across your head?"

"Well, Peter, I have read about that."

"Well, that's exactly where I am and I am sitting here in an enormous amount of stress and fear, and I can't put my finger on it. I don't know why I am so afraid, can you come over?"

"Well, yes Peter, I can."

help them to understand and to accept. The visiting care-givers can be a link between the sick person, the family and friends, in order to establish or re-establish communications before the time of death arrives.

The principal objective for the care-giver can always be to help persons who are sick to use well the time that remains. This would include assisting them to put in order their tempo-

I got there about an hour later, and I sat down with Peter, and he said: "Irene, I have so much fear, so much fear and anger."

"Peter, do you know where the anger is coming from?"

"Yes, I'm angry about the abuse of land and water."

Peter was an extremely universal person, so I took this very seriously, in a universal way, and we talked about the abuse of land and water. He talked about his fear of leaving his friends in a world where people were rejected, instead of being a community of brothers. It scared him to leave his friends in such a world. We talked universally for a while and then we pin-pointed his personal fear, which was that he wanted to leave all of his property and the little bit of money that he had to his roommate, Tom.

He had had the same roommate for thirteen years and he was afraid that his parents would come in and they would take everything from him if his will was not legal. So after a few hours we knew that his fear was of having people rip his roommate off from what he deserved.

In order to help Peter, Irene let him express his fears. She knew how to create an atmosphere of trust and security that allowed him to settle his personal affairs. The role of the care-giver is to discern the real needs of the sick person, to distinguish these from other less important desires, and to respond to the best of his or her ability.

ral affairs such as financial and legal matters. In the last phase of their illness they will have other specific needs: housing, transportation, social support. Care-givers will be able to facilitate contacts with the appropriate agencies and services when needed.

Visiting care-givers will bring support to those who have AIDS by their understanding, by their unconditional acceptance and by their hopeful presence.

107

The visiting care-giver relating with parents and friends of the sick person and with hospital personnel

Relating with parents and friends of those who are sick

Relating with hospital personnel

Both the sick person's family and hospital personnel will welcome visiting care-givers as valuable members of the health-care team.

Relating with parents and friends of those who are sick

The quality of care offered by loved ones during painful periods of illness can greatly influence the sick person's feelings of well-being and progress. Visiting care-givers can support families and friends in this task. Their role is not to substitute for close relatives and friends. Instead, their efforts should seek to improve the sick person's quality of life by assisting loved ones to offer better care.

Close relations often have a tendency to hide their feelings from their sick relatives and even from each other. They go out of their way to project a mask of good humour and a positive facade.

They can experience emotional stages, however, similar to those who are sick, and often they are ill-prepared to deal with these feelings. They, too, need to express their fears and anger, but may be unable to do so.

Visitors should know how to give of their time, showing interest for the family and winning their trust. They will thus be able to listen to the family's expressions of feelings and facilitate their efforts to unburden themselves.

Tact and balance

Visitors need both tact and discernment in order to be receptive to the confidences of others without intruding or offending them. Embarrassing situations might arise, for example, that could lead to a confrontation between family members and the sick person. In such a situation, the visitors must have a genuine respect for both parties, without becoming their arbitrator or taking sides. They can strive to show affection and disinterested love for all concerned, while maintaining a respectful emotional detachment.

Relatives must be able to count on the visitors' discretion. This confidence will further their openness and lessen their anxiety. A serene and relaxed atmosphere will also have a positive effect on the sick person's health.

An example

John is dying at 39 years of age. His wife Michelle is at his bedside with their two children: Peter, who is 10 years old, and 12-year-old Julie. Mother and children are crying. The caregiver arrives for his regular visit. He enters the room and, faced with this scene, feels completely helpless. What can he do to help?

His role is threefold:

– to help the family to face their shock;
– to provide a friendly presence and be a support at this difficult moment;
– to be available to respond to the family's specific needs.

Even if the visitor feels himself to be helpless in such a situation, his simple presence can be of tremendous benefit to the family. When sickness or death touches a family, the whole family system is affected. In such a crisis, the family often provides itself with its own defence mechanisms to cope with the situation. These defences can be healthy if they are temporary. The care-giver's support can help the family to call upon such resources in a positive way.

Three defence mechanisms

In order to survive in times of crisis, people protect themselves by anticipation, suppression and sublimation. How do these defence mechanisms work?

A husband knows that his wife is seriously ill. He envisages the loss he will undergo and prepares himself for this eventuality. Unconsciously he uses "anticipation," a defence mechanism that enables him to build a shell around himself to control these foreseen sorrows.

Another mechanism is "suppression." It prevents a person from reacting immediately to shock. The emotions arise, but they are unconsciously kept hidden because they are considered to be inappropriate in the situation, for example, crying in front of the sick person.

A third defence mechanism is "sublimation," which consists in redirecting inner impulses instead of repressing them. Different people have diverse methods of sublimating their impulses: for example, by throwing themselves into activities or by using humour. In this way they are able to cope with pressures that otherwise would be unbearable.

Visitors should not be surprised to discover that these defence mechanisms are operative among the parents and friends of those who are seriously sick. Their role can be to help these loved ones to fulfill better their supportive function with their sick relatives. "Taking the family as a unit of treatment is recognizing that the patient does not fall sick alone, and is not healed alone" (Virginia Satir).

Relating with hospital personnel

Relief for health-care personnel

When parents, friends or visitors are caring for a sick person who is anxious and constantly demanding help, they relieve health-care personnel to go about their other tasks, which are usually already very burdensome.

In the same way with the confused and agitated patient or resident who needs someone's continous presence, visiting care-givers can offer this presence and relieve health-care personnel who can occupy themselves with the needs of others who are ill.

Accepting personal helplessness

Slowly, as the years go by, I learn about the impor-tance of powerlessness. I experience it in my own life and I live with it in my work. The secret is not to be afraid of it—not to run away. The dying know we are not God. They accept that we cannot halt the process of cancer, the inexo-rable march of that terrible army that takes over a human body like an occupying force, pillaging, raping, desecrat-ing without respect and without quarter. All they ask is that we do not desert them: that we stand our ground at the foot of the cross. At this stage of the journey, of being there, of simply being: it is, in many ways, the hardest part.

Sheila Cassidy

It also happens that personnel often establish a relationship of trust with the visitors, expressing to them their own feelings of physical, moral and spiritual fatigue. Through active listening these visitors can offer them understanding and support.

A nurse, for example, is approaching a state of burn-out because of excessive pressures and overwork. By simply being listened to and understood, she can become aware herself of the changes she must make in her life. She must love herself first and take care of her own needs if she wants to be available to support her patients and their loved ones.

Visitors, finally, can be therapeutic agents within the health-care team. Within the team context, they can contribute to a better understanding of the patients, residents and their families by sharing their perceptions and helpful visiting experiences.

Knowing the limits of one's role

Hospital and nursing home volunteers receive an orientation that prepares them well for their role. But in addition to this general education, they need to be regularly informed, by those in charge of care, about the progress of patients and residents they are visiting. Such open communication with the health-care team is essential to the effective pastoral ministry of the visitors.

Visitors will guard against taking initiatives that are not their responsibility. For example:

– they will not take the patients or residents away from their floor—and still less outside the institution—without the permission of those in charge;

– they will not move them from their bed to an armchair or to a wheelchair without asking for permission, and, eventually, getting assistance;

– before giving food or drink to those who are sick, they will ensure that these conform to the diet prescribed by the physician;

– in general, they will guard against any initiatives that are the strict responsibility of the health-care personnel.

Liability insurance protects the volunteers against legal action provided their actions are in conformity with the directives of the administration of the institution where they are offering their services.

Chapter fourteen

Caring for those who are dying

The needs of the dying person

The dying person's reactions to death

Accompanying a dying person

With those afflicted by terminal illness, treatment is not intended to cure their disease but to alleviate their pain and suffering. The family and visitors in this situation have the role of complementing the health-care team in maintaining the dying person's quality of life during their final days, to the extent that this is possible.

The moments of birth and death are the most significant events in our lives: both are passages from one milieu to another, marking radical changes of state.

The true mystery of death is not, perhaps, the act of dying but our attitude toward this supremely important moment of our lives. Death gives a meaning to our existence, just as each instant of our lives has had its own meaning for us. "Death is the first question of life. Today I touch death, therefore, I ought to look for the meaning of life" (Maddly Boney).

Palliative care

The term "palliative care" refers to the unified philosophy, attitudes and treatments whose purpose is the accompaniment of dying persons during the last stage of their lives in a way that assures their respect, dignity and quality of life.

Pain and symptom control are the principal objectives of the multidisciplinary palliative care team that cares for the dying person. This team is composed of professionals from different disciplines: physicians and nurses, dieticians, physiotherapists, pharmacologists, social workers and pastoral care agents.

Within a wholistic concept of care, the different members of the team focus on diverse aspects of treatment—physical, psychological, spiritual, social, etc.—either at home or in the healthcare institution. Parents and volunteers complement the work of the palliative care team. They have the same objective:

assuring the best possible quality of life, considering the limitations imposed by the sick person's condition.

People who are dying have physical, psychological and spiritual needs that are specifically different from the needs of other bed-ridden patients. Their bodies, in fact their whole beings, are changing and adapting already to the process of death.

On the physical level

It is important to turn dying persons frequently, if their condition allows, paying special attention to the circulation of the blood in their legs.

The temperature of the body rises, even if the extremities stay cold. This elevated temperature drains the mucous membrane, especially the lips and the inside of the mouth. A glycerine ointment will relieve the lips. Moisten the mouth as often as possible.

117

The skin becomes sweaty, particularly on the upper part of the body. Dying persons customarily react to this by throwing aside their sheets. Oxygen tents are of little use in this situation.

Dying persons instinctively turn their heads toward the light. Those accompanying them are encouraged to keep themselves in their line of vision, at the head of their bed. During the last moments of life, their hearing and voices weaken, so it becomes necessary to speak clearly and distinctly, even when expressing words of tenderness and comfort.

On the psychological level

Dying persons need to live their last days in an atmosphere of security. They want to know that they will not be abandoned, that someone will be at their bedside with whom they can share their deepest feelings, confident of being understood. The presence of those they love can greatly help to lessen their anxiety.

These patients also need honesty. Those who surround them must avoid clichés and lies, even well-intentioned ones: "You seem better today...." Dying persons recognize insincerity and half-truths, for they feel in their bodies that they are not going to pull through.

On the spiritual level

Those who are dying have a pressing need to give meaning to their suffering. They need to speak of their agony and to find an answer to their question: where do we go after death? They can be supported by an understanding listener when, reviewing the events of their past lives, they feel gnawing dissatisfaction and sometimes guilt.

Faith in God and trust in God's mercy can be invaluable sources of comfort for someone who is facing death.

Visiting care-givers should be prepared to help patients who are seeking comfort from religious faith. They should be prepared to pray with them, to share with them the mysteries of life and death. If requested, they can ask for a priest, pastor, or other person with whom the dying person would like to meet.

As death approaches, those who are dying also want to retell their life stories in order to better acknowledge and accept the important events of their lives. Active listening will help them to make this review and to move into the last stage of letting go. Accepting death, finally, is saying yes to God, saying yes to the physical life that is ending.

This act of abandonment, of course, is never easy or total. As detached as one might be from all that life has bestowed, death still means a radical break with those many personal ties that have woven together to form the texture of one's life.

Religious faith does not take away the agony of death. Jesus himself experienced this agony in the Garden of Olives and on the cross: "My God, my God, why have you abandoned me?" (Matthew 27:46)

In his work, *The Dialogue of the Carmelites*, Georges Bernanos relates the death of Sister Blanche. A young religious, who had known and greatly admired Sister Blanche for her extraordinary faith, is deeply moved and astonished by her difficult death. "Who would have believed that she would undergo so much pain in dying, that she would know so poorly how to die?"

Yes, it is extremely difficult for everyone to accept limitations and finiteness. And because of this, those who are sick must pass through several stages in order to arrive at the attitude of letting go, as Elizabeth Kübler-Ross so well describes.

The dying person's reactions to death

At the moment of death, and each time that an experience of loss affects our lives, we live through five stages:

– denial and loneliness;

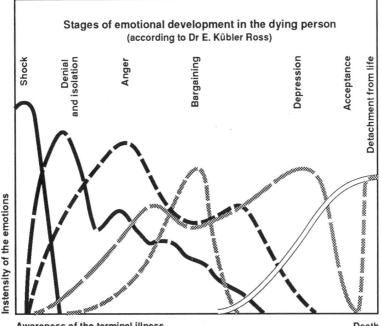

Stages of emotional development in the dying person
(according to Dr E. Kübler Ross)

Shock | Denial and isolation | Anger | Bargaining | Depression | Acceptance | Detachment from life

Instensity of the emotions

Awareness of the terminal illness   Death

- rebellion and anger;
- bargaining and camouflage;
- depression;
- acceptance.

It helps for parents and volunteers to become familiar with these stages in order to recognize better and respond to the sick person's needs. It is important to realize that these stages do not always occur in the same order and they can overlap. The feelings also do not always express themselves as clearly as we describe them here.

Denial and loneliness

The first reaction of the sick person on hearing the unwelcome news of illness is doubt and denial: "It is not possible. They are mistaken...."

This stage of denial is a normal defence mechanism when one is confronted with an upsetting event. It may not last long. Faced with the factual evidence, one usually grows to accept the reality of his or her condition. But before arriving at this point of abandonment one will pass through several other stages.

Rebellion and anger

Are not feelings of rebellion and anger an understandable reaction to sickness that unexpectedly disrupts the normal course of a person's life? Someone who has a meaningful life and plans for the future is severely jolted by a diagnosis of terminal illness.

Such persons need to express their frustrations and anger to an understanding ear. But such listening demands of the confidant a great deal of patience and moral strength. Frequently they will speak harshly of the physicians, the hospital, the health-care personnel, their own families, and of anything else that could have caused their sickness. They need to be listened to, no matter how long it takes, until they have freed themselves from these feelings weighing so heavily on their heart.

Bargaining and camouflage

In this stage the emotions give way to rationalizations and the tendency to play down the reality of the situation. Those who are sick cling to hopes of a miracle, to dreams of new medications or natural medicines that promise the slight glimpse of a cure. But the miracle is slow to come.

Here again, the visiting care-giver can accompany them in their state of expectation and questioning.

Little by little, however, the moment arrives when they ought to accept the truth of their condition and to realize that they can no longer run away. This heightened awareness is not easy and frequently leads to the next stage.

Depression

As persons who are sick face the inevitability of death they live through a painful stage drawing them to turn in on themselves. Some people sink into a profound despair leading them to contemplate committing suicide.

This stage of depression has the following characteristics: an acute awareness of approaching death and of the end of relationships with loved ones, and fear of suffering and of loneliness.

The state of the terminally ill is further aggravated by moments of discomfort and physical pain, by exhaustion and protracted weariness, and also, sometimes, by the lack of understanding on the part of relatives and friends. Here is how Y. Prigent, in *L'expérience dépressive*, describes this experience and the reactions of others to it.

"You look for someone who can help you to see more clearly, to listen to you, to hear where you are at, to be receptive to your cry of distress and to send you another message. A sign of life that can revive in you the small quivering flame that is about to go out, a gesture of complicity, of that ancient pact between the living that affirms the deepest part of one's being.

"The one who has been or will be able to be this warm mirror that does not reflect but feels, will not seek to look upon you as a problem, even as a human one, but instead to sympathize with you, to be compassionate, to 'empathize.' In brief, to feel with you what you are feeling, you, there in the whirlpool that engulfs you, him, also well soaked, with one foot on the bank and the other in the water."

Acceptance

Those who have integrated experiences of loss throughout their lives might have greater facility arriving at this stage of the acceptance of death.

Religious faith can be an invaluable support for accepting the difficult events of life and death. Is not accepting to sacrifice one's life an extraordinary act of love? Saying yes to life, just as saying yes to death, the continuity of life, is also saying yes to God.

"The act of abandonment creates a serene spirit, drives away the most persistent anxieties, softens the most bitter pains. Simplicity and freedom reign in the heart. The person with a spirit of abandonment is prepared for any eventuality. He or she is forgetful of self. This forgetfulness constitutes the death and birth in a heart that expands and dilates" (Bossuet).

Accompanying a dying person

Accompanying sick people in the terminal stage means being a mirror for them, a reflection of what they are living. In communicating with them, therefore, care-givers are to try to image their words and especially their feelings without manipulations or interventions that attempt to influence them to change their minds.

"To deceive a dying person is to lead them along a path that is not their own. It is no longer the path of their life, darkened perhaps by sickness, but whose light remains the light of their heaven" (Léon Schwartzenberg, *Requiem pour la vie*, p. 138).

This intensity of presence can allow the dying person to live each instant in a positive and creative way, no longer weighing their worth by scales of productivity and efficiency, but, instead, with full appreciation of the value of their being.

The moment of truth

What joy I experience when his glance encounters mine and tells me, with or without words: "Thank you for being there, I hope that you will be able to love me until the end."

What sadness I feel when his glance is incapable or refuses to light on mine. I know that he is suffering and alone. I know that the taming will be difficult and perhaps impossible. What fear I suffer when my glance cannot hold his for a very long time.

I recognize then my weakness, my fear, my limitations. What tension I go through when his eyes filled with rage or contempt penetrate through me and blame me for understanding nothing of his physical and moral pain. It is that look that I fear most of all. It causes me to have so many doubts and feelings of helplessness and frustration. It teaches me once more that I am not capable of taming death once and for all, since everyone must live his or her own death.

Yes, this powerful gesture of looking into the eyes of another is in touch with the truth, with the reality that is as different as is the state of those dying from that of those who are well. But it is essential if one dares to hope for a death with tenderness. If only our glance might communicate this "truth" to which dying persons have a right.

D.L.

The need for transparency

Sick people have a right to know the truth about their condition, and they expect that their visiting care-givers will be genuine with them. Let us listen to Jesus speak of this light that illumines our life:

"The lamp of your body is your eye. When your eye is sound, your whole body too is filled with light.... If, therefore, your whole body is filled with light, and there is no trace of darkness at all, it will be light entirely, as when a lamp shines upon you" (Luke 11:34, 36).

Visiting care-givers can be this light, this luminous transparency that the sick person needs. They can try to understand the world of sickness from within, in order to walk with them, to follow their rhythm. Only then can one speak of "being with," "being present" to all the dimensions of their lives.

"Life is an exchange. It is a glance acknowledged, a smile that ought to be of sympathy and never of pity. It is a word that ought to be frank and never false" (Schwartzenberg, *Requiem pour la vie*, p. 156).

Accompaniment is certainly an affair of the heart. But it is still necessary to know sick persons well: what they have been, their roles in society and their relationships with their families.

The objective of the visitor is to bring to those who are dying the serenity they need to make the passage from life to death. Certainly there are no ready-made recipes. The companions of sick persons must discover for themselves the meaning and intensity of the relationships they will establish with those they are visiting.

The tenderness of gestures

Christiane Jomain, author of *Mourir dans la tendresse*, had an extraordinary attitude! She knew how to say what I myself had noticed: "The spirit with which the body is cared for contributes to moral support and has a psychological and social effect on the patient."

Gestures of tenderness that combine both care and support are the only way of using well the limited time available. Bath time becomes sacred, precious. Slow and gentle movements communicate to the patient our recognition that he or she is a valuable, vibrant human being.

In the autumn of 1983 I decided to work with dying persons. I had reflected a great deal about the reasons inspiring me to choose to work among the "lepers" of a society that denies the "sickness of death" from which it is suffering. It is my spiritual journey that led me to palliative care: I wanted to share with those who are dying the hope of Jesus resurrected. I knew well that it wasn't a question of preaching or conversions. I ought to be like Jesus since he was living in me. It would mean trying to reveal his loving presence by my manner of being and acting.

I had decided to concentrate all my attention and concern while I was washing the feet of my patients. I was hoping to have the same interior attitude that Jesus himself would have had on Holy Thursday night.

I bent to my knees in order to wash and dry their feet. I always finished by oiling both feet, massaging them to relax, strengthen, ease, hand over... I often lacked the time to do more, but the washing of the feet was indispensable because of the spirit with which I did it.

At the end of forty-two months, of hundreds of feet and five times more of toes, a patient gave me certain proof of my "theory." He was an elderly Jewish convert who said to me, with deep emotion (crying), while I was washing his feet in a basin: "But...that makes me think of Lord Jesus!"

D.L.

125

Chapter fifteen

Practical information for those who are terminally ill

The rights of sick persons

The living will

Funeral arrangements

F amilies of those who are terminally ill have great difficulty taking care of the final arrangements as the moment of death approaches. It is painful for them to bring up the subject since it seems to confirm for their sick relative and for themselves that death is imminent. Frequently the family will turn to the social worker or the visitor to help them with these delicate tasks.

Persons who are dying should be encouraged to draw up a will, if they have not already done so, in order to avoid any problems of succession or inheritance. In situations where they are open and accepting of their condition, they might like to plan their own funeral and burial arrangements.

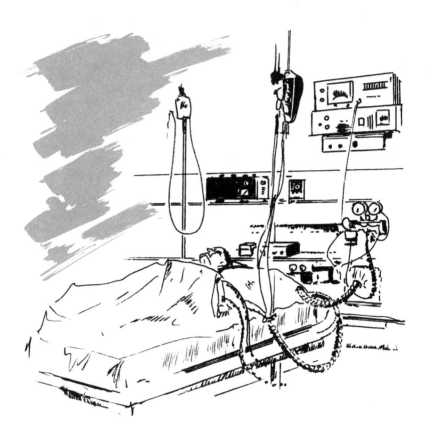

The fact of involving the dying person in these decisions will confirm for them that their rights and last wishes are being respected.

The rights of sick persons

Sick persons have a greater tendency to take responsibility for their own care, choosing or refusing the therapy offered, if they are independent and given the opportunity to decide.

Their needs become greater once they know with certainty that they will not recover and that death is inevitable. They wish, then, to have greater control over their symptoms and treatments in order to live as comfortably and as lucidly as possible the remaining days of their lives.

The right to die

A care-giver with those seriously ill has said: "In my opinion, every human being has the right to die. Not only to die, but to leave this stage of life with serenity and support, and not with all these treatments that, to my mind, are often useless, unnecessary and painful for the sick person. I find that we make them suffer more by not telling them clearly their real condition. Many of those dying realize they are about to die only at the last minute and do not receive the spiritual care they need."

We are beginning to realize, states Dr. David Roy (director of the Institute of Bioethics, Montreal) that sick persons themselves, if they are conscious, are the authorities in the dying process. The physician has a certain scientific authority with respect to the administration of medication, but only the persons who are the principal actors in the drama have the authority to say: "I want all these treatments to end; I refuse to be surrounded by all these machines. Let me now die in peace."

The role of the visitor

Watching sick people die can be very painful for visitors who have grown to know and love them. But if these visitors are aware of the importance of respecting the sick person's rights, they will not try to change their minds about dying, even though this can demand a great deal of tact.

It is sometimes impossible to know if those who are sick truly desire to die, or if they want all the technical means available to be used to prolong a life that is already seriously debilitated. If they are unconscious, and they have not indicated what their preference would be, then the decision must be made in consultation with family and/or significant others. A common sense orientation, without other clear guidelines, would dictate that a person would prefer to live rather than to die, as long as it would not imply undue pain, inconvenience or financial expense. Physicians are never obliged to take extraordinary means to prolong the life of the terminally ill.

Such is the orientation given in 1957 by Pope Pius XII during an allocution to anaesthetists: the physician is not morally obliged to use extraordinary means in order to preserve life and health. These terms have been given various interpretations. "Ordinary" would be treatment that would offer a reasonable hope of success without entailing disproportionate suffering for the sick person. "Extraordinary," on the other hand, would be treatment that would not offer reasonable expectations for recovery or relief, and which would entail considerable suffering.

The right to die, therefore, is a right of every person. This right is recognized but not imposed: no person or institution has the role or power to appropriate the death of another.

Beginning in 1970, a trend developed in the United States to protect the right of sick people to die with dignity. A law, entitled the "Natural Death Act," was passed in California, allowing those who are sick to make a written directive stipulating that, if they are afflicted by an incurable illness and are unable to communicate their wishes, they do not intend to benefit from artificial means of prolonging life, as this is defined by the law. To date no such legislation exists in Canada.

This procedure has been called the "living will." It consists of a written document signed by a responsible adult, who is not necessarily sick or undergoing medical care. This procedure can take the form of simple instructions left with the family, or of a formal document signed before a notary.

Those who sign such a document state their desire that, if one day they are no longer capable of expressing their wishes about proposed treatment, the treatment will not automatically be given. Dr. Monet has clearly expressed the implications of such action: "The quality of a person's remaining days are more important than their quantity. The patient has the choice of living a little longer and less well, or a shorter time and better."

Value of the living will

The living will is a valuable expression of personal intentions, but its practical application requires considerable discernment. When are we sure that the sickness is terminal? There are surprising cases of remission followed by several years of meaningful life. When is treatment considered to be extraordinary? Would it also include intravenous feeding? When is it necessary to remove the life-support systems?

Faced with all of these questions, there will always be a need for dialogue among the health-care team, the family, the volunteers. Within this context, the document signed by the dying person and witnesses is very important in deciding what action to take.

The quality of life

Underlying these life and death decisions is the concept of "quality of life," a concept about which it is difficult to give objective norms. We all define it from our own life experiences, desires and the meaning that we give to life.

But it is clear that for some persons in the final phase of a terminal illness, prolongation of life secures only a precarious and burdensome existence. For Christians and for many other people of faith, as we will see in the fourth part of this work, these final days can open up new perspectives on the sanctity of human life.

The testament of my end of life

(Example of a living will)

From the moment where I will not be able to express myself and where the treatment would not guarantee a sufficient recovery of my physical capacities and of my mental faculties,

I the undersigned:

refuse to be kept alive by medication, machines or artificial and disproportionate means.

I desire that medication be given to me to effectively control my pain, even if this causes me to die more quickly. I ask for myself a peaceful, natural, dignified death.

Every decision concerning a medical intervention ought to be discussed with myself, if possible, and with those who have been my witnesses, before its application. The names of the witnesses who will stand in for me in case I become incapacitated are listed below.

These last wishes for the end of my life are drawn up after mature reflection and ought to be respected in the same way as a will.

Those who will be taking care of me ought to feel morally bound to follow these directions. I ask them to have no feelings of guilt in my regard since today I officially assume entire and complete responsibility for this action.

(Signature of the person and of two witnesses, with the date.)

(On the reverse of the form further explanations can be added under the following heading: *"Now that I know the nature of the illness I have, I am leaving here specific instructions on the manner of treating me for the future and rest of my life."* New signatures of the person and the witnesses, with the date, are needed with these instructions.)

This document, which does not have legal authority, is now distributed in many health-care centres.

Visiting care-givers may be asked to assist the family with the funeral details, or even to make all of the arrangements themselves if the family is at a distance.

Arrangements at the time of death

If the person has died at home, the body ought to be transported immediately to the hospital so that a physician can certify death. He or she will also judge if there ought to be a coroner's inquest. Afterward, the funeral parlour will take possession of the body.

Several decisions must be made at this point, in conformity with the wishes expressed by the sick person before death:

–   to choose a funeral parlour (also to be considered is whether the person has chosen to have an open coffin);

–   to make arrangements for the burial or cremation;

–   to determine with the parish the time for the funeral and to plan the ceremony (and to decide if the ceremony will take place with the body present);

–   if necessary, to gather together the papers required for finalizing the succession, insurance, etc. The visitors can help the family to fill out the necessary forms or indicate resource persons and organizations that could be of assistance.

Support for the family

Visitors can offer much needed support during these emotional times. Their presence at the wake and at the funeral can provide comfort for the family and help them in the important process of integrating their grief.

Because of the ties that the visitors have created with the sick persons and their loved ones, they are often invited to stay in contact with the members of the family to help during the grieving period. They will thus be able to put the most seriously affected members in contact with organizations that can respond to their needs; for example, groups for grief therapy.

Part four

Spiritual accompaniment

Chapter sixteen

The spiritual needs of those who are sick

Difficulties sick persons must face

A reassuring presence

Crises as opportunities for growth

A deepening interiority

With their need for physical and psychological care, sick persons require moral and spiritual support.

This support can be provided by visiting care-givers, whose loving presence can help them to enter more deeply within themselves to discover there the mystery of the divine presence. Did not Jesus say, "The Kingdom of God is within you"?

Spiritual accompaniment requires of care-givers the qualities of availability, patience, openness to life and a spirit of hope. When sick persons express their desire to enter more profoundly into themselves and to find meaning in their lives, visitors can be companions with them on this journey.

When their discomforts drag on and become burdensome, when symptoms worsen and turn into serious illnesses, when their condition becomes terminal and they must prepare for death, sick persons feel themselves to be alone and distraught.

They must then find within themselves the capacity to face all of these difficulties that afflict them. But how? Visitors can help them to find deep within themselves this Source of life, this God who is always present and who loves them unconditionally.

Job, the saintly figure from the Old Testament, has articulated well the anguish that pursues those who are seriously afflicted:

> "My kindred and my most intimate friends
> have all gone away,
> and the guests in my house have forgotten me.
> The serving maids treat me as a foreigner,
> a stranger, never seen before.
> My servant does not respond to me when I call him,
> I am reduced to entreating him.
> To my wife my breath is unbearable,
> for my own brothers I am a thing corrupt.
> Even children look down on me,
> whenever I appear, they greet me with a jibe.
> All my dearest friends recoil from me in horror:
> those I loved best have turned against me.
> Beneath my skin, my flesh begins to rot,
> and my bones stick out like teeth.
> Pity me, pity me, you, my friends,
> for God's hand has struck me."

(Job 19:14-21)

In such distress the sick can find strength in the Word of God that gives meaning to their suffering and to their approaching death. It can sooth their anguish and help them to say YES to all that happens in their lives, both in the difficult days and in the happy ones.

The Word of God

I have been crucified with Christ. I now live not with my own life but with Christ's life within me. The life I now live in this body I live in faith: faith in God's Son who loved me and who sacrificed himself for my sake.

(Galatians 2:19-20)

All I want is to come to know Christ and the power of his resurrection and to share his sufferings by reproducing the pattern of his death. That is how I can hope to take my place in the resurrection of the dead.... Forgetting the past, I strain ahead for what is still to come; I race for the finish to win the prize which God calls us upward to receive in Christ Jesus.

(Philippians 3:10-12, 13-15)

Indeed, as the sufferings of Christ overflow into our lives, so also, through Christ, does our consolation overflow.... And our hope for you is secure, since we know that, sharing our sufferings, you will also share our consolations.

(2 Corinthians 1:5, 6, 7)

And if we are children we are also heirs: heirs of God and co-heirs with Christ, provided that we share his sufferings so as to share his glory. I think that what we suffer now can never be compared to the glory, as yet unrevealed, which is waiting for us.

(Romans 8:17-18)

A reassuring presence

In moments of deep desolation, those who are sick hardly need words. They need, instead, a reassuring presence that understands their anguish and accepts them. Visitors who have already lived themselves through such desolation can be a great support, just as it was written about Jesus:

"... because he has himself been tempted he is able to help others who are tempted as well" (Hebrews 2:18).

After accompanying someone through this stage of illness, Father Angelo Busco, in his work *Amour et service,* related the type of presence that was possible to him: "I found no other means of relieving Aubin's psychological and spiritual

137

sufferings except by my silent presence, with discrete and appropriate reflections, with understanding and sharing, in constant fidelity, despite the hesitations and resistances."

This presence can also take the form of specific gestures: a reading the sick have chosen, listening to peaceful music (some music cassettes are a very effective therapy for both heart and spirit), a spontaneous prayer adapted to the situation, a gift of flowers, a card or even a simple glass of water. All of these gestures are signs of God's love for his suffering sons and daughters.

Crises as opportunities for growth

When sickness strikes, those afflicted are thrown into confusion as was Paul on the road to Damascus. They lose the sense of security on which they have based their lives. They see themselves without masks, with all of the limitations that their condition imposes on them.

Sickness brings its own procession of stresses and anxieties. With the help of understanding care-givers, however, persons who are sick can release these tensions. Gradually they can arrive at a state of calm and serenity that facilitates the healing process or at least makes their lives less burdensome. Some of those afflicted by sickness enter into an aggressive stage, blaming everyone around them for their ills. These people do not need consoling words or encouragement to accept their condition. They simply want someone to be there for them, someone close, to accept what they are feeling. If they can freely express their frustrations and anger, they can arrive at a point of freeing themselves and even of finding a new personal expansion in this difficult stage of their lives.

Each crisis becomes an opportunity for growth, especially if it is lived in an atmosphere of acceptance, without any judgment or blame from others. It must be admitted that the visitors' vocation is not always easy, but if the visitor is able to establish good relations with sick people and gain their confidence, amazing things will happen.

A deepening interiority

Often enough, sickness occasions an interior renewal. You might notice, for example, that after several weeks of severe suffering, those you are visiting have a new vision of life that reflects a return to essentials.

They have given up many false and superficial values. Their sickness has been like a key unlocking the mysteries of the interior life, or, as psychologist Carl Jung has said, inviting them "to give up superficial being in order to penetrate always

138

more into one's inner depths." A young motorcyclist, paralysed due to an accident, confessed: "You are going to be surprised to hear me say this, but it has been the opportunity of my life; I was a human wreck, I have become someone."

Spiritual accompaniment facilitates the discovery of Christ within oneself. Saint Augustine prayed to the Lord, in his *Confessions:* "So long have I sought you outside myself, when you were so close, within me."

Helping someone to find their deepest Source: is that not the goal of spiritual accompaniment of the sick?

Thank you for being there, Lord

When life has become a chore,
when our nights are disturbed by nightmares,
thank you for being there, Lord,
and for being present to us.

When we are alone and forgotten,
when we are afraid of loving and being loved,
thank you for being there, Lord,
and for offering us your love.

When sickness strikes,
when trials are heavy to carry,
thank you for being there, Lord,
and for extending your hand.

When we have lost hope,
when blackness fills the horizon,
thank you for being there, Lord,
and for bringing us your light.

Rev. Normand Provencher, OMI

Chapter seventeen

Faith
in a God of love

Faith means saying yes to God

A new dynamic life

Toward peace and serenity

A meaning for life and death

Living the Paschal Mystery with Jesus

During their long nights of insomnia and days of inactivity, sick people become preoccupied with fundamental questions of life such as: Why all this suffering? Why is it happening to me? What is the reason, finally, for human life?

And almost inevitably the question of God arises from within their heart and spirit: Who is God? Is God really interested in us?

Faith means saying yes to God

Faith in God is more than simply believing in some truth we have learned. The well-known German theologian Walter Kasper, who has seriously studied this question, has written:

"Faith does not mean only holding something to be true. Nor is it a matter of simple confidence. Believing means saying AMEN to God, strengthening ourselves in him and leaning on him for support. Believing means letting God be totally God, acknowledging him as the unique reason and meaning of our lives. Faith, therefore, is to exist in receptivity and obedience."

Having faith in God, therefore, means saying YES, abandoning ourselves confidently into God's hands, handing over to him our sufferings, our joys, our entire lives.

Believing in God is having the conviction that we are precious in God's eyes, even if we are unable to do anything, even if we have difficulty praying. We are always God's children, even if we are sick, elderly, or weak. We offer ourselves to him in total abandonment.

This handing over of ourselves to God is the fruit of the heart: those who love and who have been loved understand and accept without too much difficulty that God loves them and wishes their well-being, even in the midst of great trials. This emphasizes the importance of having lived experiences of true love in order to attain a true image of a loving God. Often those who are present to sick persons will be able, by their sensitive and loving attitudes, to help them to reach this truer perception of God.

Saying yes to a loving God is also abandoning ourselves to the present moment, certain that whatever is happening to us at this time is best for us. Like Charles de Foucauld, the humble hermit of the Sahara desert, we have the courage to say: "May your will be done, Lord. I desire only what you want and I abandon myself over to you."

A new dynamic life

This abandonment is not synonymous with resignation. The gesture of letting go brings about the relaxation of one's whole being; it leads to intimacy with God. The great bishop Bossuet has written about abandonment:

"Abandonment creates a serene spirit, it drives away the most lively anxieties, soothes the most bitter pains. Simplicity and freedom reign in the heart. The person with this spirit of abandonment is prepared for any eventuality; one is forgetful of oneself. This self-forgetfulness is the death and birth in one's heart that expands and dilates."

Practically speaking, for those who are seriously ill, this abandonment means living fully the present moment: why wish to anticipate the future? Such expectations will bring only apprehension and anguish. Living each day at a time, without

142

futile worrying about tomorrow, is the secret of a new dynamic life, for it allows one to live totally the present moment.

Toward peace and serenity

How is it possible to know peace and serenity while my being is wasting away and my death is imminent?

Those who are seriously ill live intensely three kinds of agony: the loneliness of abandonment, the denial of their deterioration, and the despair felt faced with the seeming absurdity of their lives. Many times when visiting care-givers help the sick person to express deeply hidden feelings, these three concerns rise to the surface.

The secret of serenity and even of joy, in these critical moments, is handing everything over to God in a generous act of abandonment: body, spirit, heart, one's entire life. Those who abandon themselves in this way into the hands of the

143

Father, the one who has bestowed on them the inestimable gift of life, are able to let go of every resistance. They discover within themselves a deep peace and a gentle serenity. Let us listen to Ignace Larranaga describe for us one stage of this transformation.

"Take a relaxing position, quieten your spirit. Be present to the Lord, in faith. Focus your attention on your present ills, on those that preoccupy you or that you fear. Hold your attention on each one; accept them in the mystery of the will of the Father, one by one, slowly...until your fears disappear and you begin to experience an all-pervasive peace" (*Montre-moi ton visage*).

Certain psalms express the same sentiments using the image of the good shepherd, who loves and protects each of his sheep.

> *"Yahweh is my shepherd,*
> *I shall not want.*
> *In pastures of green grass he lets me lie....*
> *Though I pass through a dark valley,*
> *I fear no harm;*
> *beside me your rod and your staff*
> *are there, to comfort me....*

Surely goodness and kindness shall follow me,
every day of my life;
my home is the house of Yahweh,
for as long as I live!

(After Psalm 23)

This psalm is an act of total surrender into the hands of the Lord: what security and what peace are expressed here! What faith and vital energy resonate between the lines; what joy in living.

A meaning for life and death

For those who are sick, as for those who accompany them in their joys and sorrows, the question of the meaning of life usually arises, at times in an obsessive way.

When we are in good health, when everything is going well, we hardly ever ask this question. Except perhaps during long nights of insomnia or on those mornings when the events of the evening before have left our mouths bitter. Then we question obsessively and anxiously the fundamental meaning of our lives and our final destiny. Even for those of us who believe ourselves to be firmly anchored in this area of our lives, serious sickness can soon shake these solid convictions.

When people who are sick live through painful experiences that they judge to be negative and destructive, they need help to integrate these experiences and to give them meaning. It will often be the role of the visiting care-givers to facilitate this process: by their availability, their active listening, their unconditional love, they can assist sick persons to discover for themselves their own truth.

It is practically a waste of time to lecture sick people, to strongly advise them, to try to convince them with persuasive arguments. Only they themselves can discover their own truth. We can simply assist them to enter into themselves in order to encounter there the Spirit of Jesus who already speaks to their hearts. They carry the solution within themselves and our role is that of a facilitator in this quest of interiority.

(We will see in the next chapter how to guide sick people and to accompany them in faith and prayer.)

Living the Paschal Mystery with Jesus

For Christians who live their faith in a committed way, their awareness of Jesus Christ is a source of comfort and hope. Encountering the Lord with the aid of a spiritual companion

can assist them to find the meaning of their sufferings, of their past lives and, perhaps, of their approaching death.

For long periods of time they contemplate Jesus who loves them unconditionally and accepts to give his life in order to be faithful to his mission. He also meets with the failure of death, but the light of his resurrection gives them the certitude that all suffering does have meaning and is a bearer of hope. Bonhoeffer has written from the horrors of a Nazi concentration camp: "Joy is hidden in suffering, as life is hidden in death." This joy Bonhoeffer had experienced in union with the resurrected Christ, and he writes about it throughout his admirable works.

It must be admitted that this discovery is not easy; it can require a long and painstaking journey. Like the disciples on Easter morning, we can arrive at this certitude that all suffering is not in vain. We can experience in our lives that suffering can be a source of interior growth. The acceptance of sickness, of suffering and, finally, of death can lead us to a deepened awareness of the wisdom of God. This discovery results from fidelity to love, from persistent faith in this God who asks only that we turn to him in simplicity of heart.

Good News for the sick

Sickness will always be with us in our world, even if the amazing progress of medicine continues.

But Jesus has given a new meaning to sickness. We can no longer claim that it is a punishment and penalty sent by God. Even more, we can be certain that God does not abandon those who are sick, that they are always his children, destined for a better world of which Jesus gave us a glimpse by his physical and spiritual healings.

Even more than having cured sick people, Jesus identified himself with them in a real and mysterious way. He clearly said: "I was sick and you visited me" (Matthew 25:36). This good news is a light and a comfort for all who are sick, and it encourages those in good health to visit them, to assist them with their healing, to accompany them.

Rev. Normand Provencher, OMI

Chapter eighteen

Prayer

What is prayer?

Praying with those who are sick

Different kinds of prayer

The sacraments for the sick person

The sick person's prayer

An elderly woman, very seriously ill, testified to the importance of prayer during the last stage of her life:

"My sickness has been a source of gratitude for me. It has alerted me to my approaching death. And this is a grace, because now I can prepare myself knowing what the future holds. I have been able to receive the Anointing of the Sick during the celebration of the Mass with my family present at my home.

"What peace, what joy to receive this final comfort in full possession of my faculties, surrounded by the love of my friends, my children and grandchildren."

(Translated from J. T. Catoir,
Le Seigneur est ma joie, p. 75)

This moving text helps us to appreciate the beneficial effects of prayer, especially when it is experienced in a loving atmosphere and as part of the Church's celebration. Her words witness also to the inner peace that prayer can bring to the spirit and heart of the sick person.

What is prayer?

When we pray we turn to God, we lift up our minds and hearts to God. Prayer is a heart-to-heart encounter with the God who loves us.

As in any other encounter with a friend or loved one, prayer includes moments of silence and moments of attentive listening for the signs of God's love and concern for us. It also includes speaking to God from our hearts and out of the depths of our feelings. All the feelings that we experience daily — our hopes, fears, anger, joys and sorrows — can be shared in this conversation with God.

We pray to draw closer to God, to derive strength and direction from the divine energy that gives us life. We pray to know ourselves better, to have greater truth in our lives. We pray always with the conviction that it is the Spirit dwelling within us who teaches us how to pray.

The Lord responds to all our prayers. The sick person who prays for healing perhaps may not receive exactly what he or she is seeking. God's response, instead, may be an unexpected spiritual or emotional healing or the grace of light and strength to accept and grow through whatever happens.

This beautiful song of the prophet Isaiah (41:9-10) expresses well the Lord's attitude toward us:

You whom I have brought
from the remotest parts of the world
and have called from the ends of the earth;
you to whom I said, "You are my servant,
I have chosen you, not rejected you"...
do not be so full of fear, for I am with you;
stop being anxious or alarmed, for I am your God.
I give you strength, I bring you help,
I hold you firmly in my victorious right hand.

The spirit of prayer

Praying with and for the sick person requires of the care-giver a prayerful attitude. Fundamental to this attitude is the conviction that Jesus is present and is still at work healing his people today. He has chosen us with all of our unique strengths and weaknesses to manifest his presence to those whom we visit.

When we pray with someone who is sick we are not alone: "For where two or three gather in my name, I shall be with them" (Matthew 18:20). Jesus' healing power and love is there to give strength and light.

This attitude is shown when we encourage the sick person to pray with great confidence. Because Jesus is concerned about their sufferings, he wants them to pray for what they desire and need. They can pray to be healed, to have a successful opera-tion, to feel less pain or to be freed from depression.

At the same time we can help them to understand that their desires and hopes are in the hands of God who alone knows what is best. As Jesus prayed in Gethsemane before his crucifix-ion, "Abba (Father), you can do all things. Take this cup away from me. But let it be as you would have it, not I." (Mark 14:36) Likewise, the prayer of the sick and of the well is ultimately that God's will be done.

We express this prayerful attitude when, at the beginning of a day of visiting or before entering a patient's room, we acknowledge the presence of the Lord and bring to mind the patients we will be meeting today. We might use a psalm or a short prayer adapted to our particular situation. An example could be:

Lord I believe in your presence and love.

Give me a spirit of compassion to enter
into places of pain.

Help me to accept my own brokenness
and my need for healing.

And grant that all of my efforts today may be filled
with your peace and wisdom. Amen.

This prayerful attitude also implies that we, as care-givers, are convinced of the importance of prayer for our own spiritual growth and nourishment. Praying with those we visit must flow from the depths of our own prayer life. Our prayer minis-try will be most effective when we are prayerful ourselves.

A pastoral visit frequently offers the opportunity for praying with the sick person. Such moments of prayer can be deep experiences of communion, sources of interior healing and peace.

Talking about prayer or saying a prayer, however, are not necessary in order for a visit to be pastoral. A visit does not become pastoral simply because a prayer is said. Prayer, or God-talk (which means using religiously oriented words), in fact, can sometimes be used by care-givers to avoid serious or painful dialogue.

Some guidelines

There are few general rules that can dictate what should be done in particular circumstances. Always praying with those who are sick, or never praying with them, are equally inappropriate practices.

Prayer is a very personal experience. It doesn't mean the same thing to everyone. Most of us have learned to pray when we were very young, and we have become comfortable with certain types of personal prayer and church rituals. What is meaningful to us now usually relates to what we have learned at an early age.

Care-givers must always try to be attentive to the physical, emotional and spiritual needs of the sick person at the time of the visit. This attentiveness is the cardinal rule.

Does this person want to pray at this time? If so, with which types of prayer is she or he most comfortable? Formal or spontaneous prayer? Biblical texts or reflections for meditation? Silent prayer? Reception of a sacrament? Are non-verbal gestures welcomed? It is well to note the person's physical condition of pain or fatigue, or lack of privacy, etc. Often enough a short well-known prayer will be most appropriate.

Religious traditions

It helps to know the religious orientations of those we are visiting. Attitudes to prayer and devotional practices vary among religions and from one Christian denomination to another. Even someone who has not practised his or her religion for many years will often wish, in the crisis of sickness, to return to devotions learned as a child in church.

Members of Protestant denominations are usually familiar with spontaneous prayer. They use the Scriptures for their devotionals, but not usually a prayer book. The Lord's Prayer is

familiar to all Christians. For Presbyterians of an older genera-
tion, the King James version of the Bible should be used and
references to God should be in terms of "Thee" and "Thou."
The surest source of prayer for a Jewish patient is the Psalms.
Most Roman Catholics appreciate formal prayers such as the
Lord's Prayer, Hail Mary, Glory Be, Acts of Faith, Hope and
Charity, and the Rosary. And both Anglicans and Roman
Catholics turn to the sacraments as an important source of
nourishment in moments of crisis.

How to lead prayer

When the care-giver knows that a patient wants to pray, but
is not sure what he or she prefers, it can be helpful simply to ask
or suggest what method to use: "Judith, when we pray together, what would you say to our beginning with a few
moments of silent prayer? Each of us could pray quietly in our
own hearts. Then, I'll pray out loud, and if you wish, you could
add your own prayers. When we are finished we could end
with an Our Father. Does that sound O.K.?"

After praying together, you could sometimes offer the sick
person an opportunity to discuss the thoughts and feelings
experienced during prayer. This will give guidance for subse-
quent prayer times together. It will also reveal feelings that the
person might wish to explore further:

Care-giver: "John, I'm wondering what you were
thinking while we were praying together."

John: "When you mentioned my daughter, I felt sad
and a little guilty that I haven't been as good a father as I
should have been."

Care-giver: "If you want we could talk about your
feelings, your sadness and guilt."

God is always present and active in each of our visits,
whether or not we use religious words or prayers. Our own
faith in God's active presence will help us to discern if it is a
good moment to pray with the sick person and how to do it.

Different kinds of prayer

Praying during a visit should arise naturally from the tone
of the visit itself. The concerns discussed, the feelings expressed
and the events that occur can all be brought to prayer. It can be
very natural, for example, for the care-giver, during a moment
of silence in the conversation, to say:

"Jim, you have been sharing with me your anxiety
about the results of the tests you have had, whether you

have cancer or not. Would you like us now to spend a few minutes in prayer, asking God for courage and strength?"

Care-givers can help those who are sick to turn simple, daily events into prayer. A person in the terminal phase of his illness, for example, was becoming annoyed by all the noises that, night and day, filled the corridors of the hospital. The care-giver wrote, with the help of patients, the following prayers related to these noises:

(A patient cries out in pain) Let us pray together for the seriously ill and despairing, for those who are tortured and persecuted, and for those tempted to commit suicide.

(A noise caused by hospital staff) Let us pray for all those who serve the sick and the elderly. May their actions be gentle and compassionate. Let us offer our sufferings in the name of all who forget to offer their lives to God.

(Shrill shouts in the street) Let us pray for those injured on the streets, in car accidents, and at work.

(A night beautiful and calm, with the window open onto the garden) Let us join ourselves to the birds' song and to all of creation in praise of the Lord.

Many patients have affirmed that this prayerful attitude has deepened their patience and sense of God's presence.

Care-givers have many resources available for praying with the sick. The following can be used and adapted to meet the needs of particular situations.

Scripture

Passages from Scripture are an especially rich source for prayer and meditation. Even those who are no longer regularly practising their religion find spiritual nourishment from passages that resonate from past memories. It is good to have bibles available for patients, since some will want them for personal spiritual reading, prayer and meditation.

A simple method for using the Bible with patients can be the following: the reading of a short scriptural passage followed by a few minutes of silent meditation and perhaps a few moments of spontaneous prayer. A patient may even want to discuss the meaning of the text as it applies to his or her present situation. The Psalms are beautiful faith-filled prayers that express the many mixed feelings experienced by those who are sick.

Formal prayers

For many of us, our introduction to prayer occurred as children when we learned such formal prayers as the Lord's

Prayer, the Hail Mary, acts of offering, of contrition, of sorrow, etc. Church attendance usually reinforced this by emphasizing the repetition of these prayers and other rituals. Using these formal prayers and rituals can bring great peace and security to someone afflicted by the disorientation of sickness.

Care-givers can always ask if the patient has a favourite prayer he or she may like to pray together. They can also use formal prayers to conclude a period of silent or spontaneous prayer, or to end a visit. If a prayer book is available for the patient to use, these prayers can be used for prayer together.

Spontaneous prayer

The term "spontaneous prayer" refers to the practice of verbally making up a prayer, adapted to a particular situation, while one is praying. The desire and ability to pray spontaneously varies with every person. For some, this type of prayer can be an unsettling experience while others take to it very naturally. For this reason it is always advisable to ask the person for her or his preference. Those from the Protestant traditions and charismatic Catholics are usually more comfortable with spontaneous prayer. Most people, even though they might not feel confident enough to pray this way themselves, appreciate a care-giver's spontaneous prayers for them.

These prayers should usually be simple, not too long, and related to the sick person's present situation:

Lord Jesus, we believe that you are present and love us.
Joan has many fears about her operation.

She fears the pain, fears that the operation may fail,
and is worried about her family.

Lord, help the doctors and nurses to do their work well.

Protect Joan's family while she is absent.

And give Joan strength and courage.

May this time of suffering lead her and her family closer to you.
Amen.

Another example is Robert, 27 years old and engaged, who is suffering from leukemia. One night he said to the care-giver: "I want to pray but I don't know what to say." The care-giver then improvised a prayer with him:

"Father, I thank you for all that Robert has experienced today. I thank you for the gift of life, for his tremendous parents, for his fiancé. You know our needs better than we do. You know Robert well: you have nurtured him from his mother's breast, you know his marriage plans and the progress of his sickness. You know that he does not find it easy to say 'Your will be done....' "

At that moment Robert signaled to stop. He raised his two hands in a sign of offering and said: "Lord, you know better than I what I need. My life, I place it in your hands, that your will may be done."

(He grasped the care-giver by the neck, tears running down his cheeks.)

Silent prayer

Prayer often rises from our hearts with no spoken words. At times no words can express the depth of feeling and longing that the human heart can hold. Such moments of silent prayer, shared in silence with another, can bring great consolation to the sick person.

The care-giver may simply hold the patient's hand or acknowledge that the Lord is present in mercy and love. Silence can then lead patient and care-giver to an experience of profound union in the Lord.

How can one pray with someone who is deaf or unable to speak, with whom communication seems almost impossible? One care-giver has suggested the following:

We had met before and had enjoyed a friendly visit. When I returned to visit Larry I placed myself before him and spoke very clearly while joining my hands: "I am going to pray with you." Then I bowed my head, in deep silence. Larry did the same. Then I took his hand and we continued to pray in silence. Larry said later that he received great consolation from this prayer, feeling close to me and to God.

Touch

Shaking a person's hand or putting your arm around another's shoulder are natural gestures of friendship. Reaching out to grasp an arm, or a hug, are spontaneous actions inspired by a desire to be close when someone is expressing emotion, whether joy or pain.

Touch is also a meaningful gesture when one is praying with another. Prayer is a personal, and often emotional, moment of closeness with God. When this closeness is shared with another through touch, the peace and communion felt usually become even more profound.

In the use of touch, the care-giver should respect the sick person's sense of privacy and intimacy. When in doubt what to do, the care-giver can always ask: "Would you like me to hold your hand while we pray?" If the patient is unconscious it can be helpful to hold his or her hand.

It is important for each care-giver to learn his or her own comfort level related to touch. Unless the care-giver feels at ease with the gesture offered, it will not be consoling for the sick person.

The laying on of hands

The New Testament emphasizes touching people when you pray, through the laying on of hands. In addition to the comfort and sense of closeness touching gives, there is a healing power in touch. Jesus invites us to make this gesture: "These are the signs that will be associated with believers... they will lay their hands on the sick who will recover" (Mark 16:17-18).

Jesus was well aware of the power of touch, for example, when he cured the woman who had suffered from a hemorrhage for 12 years: "Realizing that power had gone out from him, Jesus turned in the crowd and said, 'Who touched my clothes?' " (Mark 5:30). "People tormented by unclean spirits were also

157

cured, and everyone was trying to touch him because a power had come out of him that cured them all" (Luke 6:18-19).

In the laying on of hands, one's hands can be placed on a person's head or on the afflicted organ as one prays out loud for the person's healing. When this gesture is done in a prayerful and faith-filled way, the sick almost always experience heat and comfort. And many have related instances where this practice has resulted in healing.

If the laying on of hands is meaningful for both care-giver and sick person, this gesture can complete a period of prayer together in a deeply personal way.

Blessings

Blessings are a practice that was common to the Jewish religion. Jesus is also described blessing the children (Mark 10:13-16), his disciples (Luke 24:50-51), and food at mealtime (Mark 6:41). Through the centuries the Church has continued to encourage the use of blessings.

Blessings are prayers of praise, thanksgiving and intercession. We praise God for his goodness manifested in creation, we thank him for the continued love he shows in our lives, and we ask for his help to live our lives according to his will.

These blessings can be formalized or created for the occasion. They can be simple, a few words, or more elaborate rituals that can include some or all of the following: prayer of praise, biblical reading, short homily or reflection, prayer of thanksgiving, prayer of intercession, and hymns to begin and end the ceremony. The essential elements can be found in the eucharistic liturgy which is itself the most perfect blessing.

Blessings can be prayerful ways of celebrating with God meaningful events of life. Such occasions could include the following: with parents before and after childbirth, after a baby or child has died, on the anniversary of the death of a loved one, before and after surgery, when learning that one's illness is terminal.

All of the elements of the blessing — the readings, prayers and reflections — should relate to the sick person's situation. And whenever possible, it is good for the sick person and family to be involved in the preparations. These blessings offer great opportunity for creativity and personal meaning for those who participate in them.

Two examples of very simple general blessings are given below.

Lord Jesus, our Saviour and brother,
we praise you and thank you for your

goodness and love.
Listen to our prayers;
look with love on Tom and
help him in this time of sickness.
Bless him with the gifts of your Spirit.
Grant him the courage to carry his cross
and bring him back to full health and strength.
Lord Jesus, we ask this grace in your name. Amen.

And: (Putting your hand on the sick person's head)

May God bless you, Mary,
and help you to get better soon.
In the name of the Father, and of the Son,
and of the Holy Spirit.
(All answer) *Amen.*

The sacraments for the sick person

Christians never really pray alone. As members of the community of believers in Jesus Christ, we pray always as part of that community. The church of Jesus Christ is a community of prayer, of suffering, of service and of fellowship. And, in the Spirit, each of us shares in differing degrees in the full life of that community.

This community dimension of prayer is expressed most fully in the celebration of the sacraments. Through the Church's sacraments, the events of our individual lives become part of the life of the larger believing community. This gives our own lives new meaning.

For those who are sick, the celebration of the sacraments can be an occasion for deepening their awareness of how interdependent they are, of how much they need others, and of the love that the community bears toward them.

Certain sacraments are particularly consoling for the sick person. Even when these are administered only by a priest or a deacon, care-givers often have an opportunity to prepare the patients for the sacrament and to create the atmosphere needed to make of it a meaningful and personal celebration.

Reconciliation

The suffering and dislocation that accompany sickness frequently put those who are sick in touch with the broken relationships in their lives. Feelings of guilt and long-standing wounds can reappear. And they can feel a deep longing to be reconciled — with God, with loved ones, and with themselves.

Care-givers who are sensitive to these deeper yearnings and needs can help the sick person to express these painful

159

feelings. Through an attitude of empathic listening and acceptance, they can lead them to an experience of forgiveness.

This can also be focussed in prayer:

Lord, our Saviour,
You know the sorrow and guilt in Sarah's heart.
Enter into her pain, touch her hidden wounds
and be for her a healing presence of forgiveness.
Help her to know you as her loving and forgiving Saviour.
We ask this, Lord Jesus, in your name. Amen.

When a patient wants to receive the sacrament of reconciliation, the care-giver can help to make it a prayerful experience.
The patient may need help preparing, making an examination
of conscience, deepening his or her trust in God. The care-giver
may also assist by calling a priest and providing a place that is
private for the celebration.

Communion for the sick person

The reception of Holy Communion, even when received
alone in a hospital bed, unites one to the community of believers. This celebration is a personal encounter with Christ and
with the believing community, since it is a continuation of the
Eucharist celebrated in community.

Care-givers can help to create a prayerful atmosphere by
preparing a table near the bed and by drawing curtains for
intimacy. They can read a scripture passage and help the sick
person to reflect on God's forgiveness and his many blessings.
After communion, they can continue the thanksgiving by leading prayers for the sick person, for loved ones and for all those
suffering in the world. Prayer books with suggestions for each
part of this ceremony are available.

Since sickness can be such an isolating experience, it is
important to emphasize the community dimension of this celebration of communion.

The Anointing of the Sick

This sacrament can be administered to anyone with a serious illness, to those about to undergo serious surgery, and to
those in a weakened condition due to old age.

Although the Anointing of the Sick is administered by a
priest or deacon, the care-giver may be the best person to set up
the physical location with candles, flowers, etc., and to create a
prayerful atmosphere for those who will be present. Relatives
and friends can be encouraged to be present when this is
convenient and the sick person so desires. These people repre-

sent the community of believers praying with and for the sick person.

Prayer cards and books with the anointing rite can be made available to all present to ensure greater understanding and participation.

Communion for the dying person

Viaticum, which means food for the road, is the sacrament of communion given to those who are dying. It can be received as part of the Anointing of the Sick, during the celebration of the Eucharist, or at an appropriate moment outside of these ceremonies. The role of the care-giver is very much determined by the circumstances, and what has been written above can be applied here when appropriate.

The sick person's prayer

Prayer with those who are ill has as its ultimate goal to facilitate their own prayer. During the long days and nights of illness they have the opportunity to engage in a long dialogue with the Lord, to nourish themselves and to be consoled by his presence and love.

When the subject of prayer comes up during a pastoral visit, patients sometimes say, "I don't know how to pray" or "I don't think that God hears my prayers." These comments can come from many sources, including feelings of personal inadequacy and misconceptions about prayer.

Most people pray more often and better than they realize. Care-givers can assist sick persons to appreciate that prayer rises from the many feelings that they carry in their hearts daily. They can assure them that the simple desire to pray is already prayer. There are no "right words" that must be said. And though God always responds, his response is not always as fast as we expect, or in the way we expect.

Many people pray when they are alone in their beds, in silence. But unfortunately, they often don't realize that they are praying and how close God is to them.

Care-givers can provide patients with bibles, rosaries, prayer cards and booklets with prayers for different occasions. When the moment is right, they can talk with them about prayer, and even teach methods of prayer and meditation.

Most importantly, care-givers can encourage those who are sick to adopt a prayerful attitude and a faith-filled conviction that the Lord loves them and is present for them with his healing grace.

As relatives, friends or volunteers, we are invited to pray for those we visit. Many of them will ask us to pray for them. And even when they don't ask, we ought to pray because we believe that they are the suffering members of our community of faith. Those whom we visit are entrusted to our care in a special way.

As relatives, friends or volunteers, we will be an important link between the sick person and the Christian community. Those who are sick need the support and prayers of the larger community, and they will be greatly comforted to know that others are praying for them at eucharistic celebrations. The larger community, in turn, ought to be reminded of its responsibility toward its suffering members, who need the services, fellowship and prayers of the whole church.

Chapter nineteen

Living in hope

At the edge of despair

Christian hope

F or the seriously ill the future is always clouded with anxiety. They view it with uncertainty, as a threat to their happiness and survival. Their need is to find a reason to hope, in one form or another.

A sense of hope first manifests itself in terms of the survival instinct that drives them to struggle with all their energy to get well and to return to a normal life. If this life force weakens, however, with no other motivation to replace it, sick persons can turn in on themselves and risk sinking into despair.

At the edge of despair

Paradoxically, both despair and suicide strike two very different types of people.

There are those who have everything, who enjoy things intensely, expecting nothing more from life. One sees youth, for example, gifted with all sorts of talents and possessions, suddenly committing suicide without apparent reason. One also sees adults sinking into despair while their lives have seemed to be total successes.

On the other extreme, there is the despair of those who do not expect more from life since for them the future is completely blocked. Some youth, some elderly, and, to be sure, some who are seriously ill, are familiar with these moments of fatal depression.

Indispensable supports

Seriously sick persons who suffer from chronic or terminal illness are those who tend to fall into this despair. For this very reason they need a great deal of support when they are being told about the seriousness of their condition.

When sickness drags on, when the discomfort and aggravation becomes unbearable, when care-givers let on that those who are sick have become a burden, depression and sometimes despair can be close at hand. When death has become certain and the period of waiting is accompanied by increased anxiety and suffering, to what can the sick person cling?

We have seen above, in the section on the five stages the sick person must face when dying, that the stage of depression is the most painful and the most difficult to overcome. When the depression is extreme and turns into despair, it can happen that the sick person dreams of suicide.

Certain extreme cases of depression, of course, that are often brought on by degeneration of the brain, can be treated with very effective medication—antidepressants—that enable the person to find a certain equilibrium.

Christian hope

A person of deep faith is an invaluable asset for those searching for meaning in these critical situations. Christian faith, for its part, offers a solid basis for a positive and confident attitude toward life and the future. Psalm One has beautifully expressed the hope that is rooted in faith in God:

Happy are those who put their faith in God,
who have made the Lord their hope.
They are like trees planted by water streams;
their roots drawing from flowing currents.
They do not suffer from the heat;
their leaves will always be green;

they will not dry up
and they will yield fruit without end.
(Adapted)

A God of love

Our hope comes from our faith in God's love. We are confident that all comes together for the best for those whom God loves. Saint Paul, who himself endured extreme torments for Christ, understood how the love of God supported him in every situation:

"All that we suffer in this life can never be compared to the glory which is waiting for us. The whole creation is eagerly waiting for God to reveal his sons and daughters....We know that the entire creation has been groaning in one great act of giving birth; and not only creation, but all of us who possess the first fruits of the Spirit are groaning inwardly as we wait for our bodies to be freed. For we must be content to hope that we shall be saved—our salvation is not in sight or we should not have to be hoping for it—but, as I say, we must still hope to be saved since we are not saved yet—we must wait for this with perseverance" (Romans 8:18-20, 22-25).

Sick people who insist on being healed at any price will fight relentlessly in order to survive. But one day they must understand that it is impossible; and even they will accept—it is hoped—that their recovery is, perhaps, not what is best for them. As these parents said when they lost Genevieve, their 17-year-old daughter: "We had thought that if Genevieve survived we would be winners, but we have finally realized that we can be winners even if she is dead."

Toward a new life

If the persons believe that God will resurrect them, and that they will see him with their own eyes of flesh, they will accept death as their birth into a new state of being. Their sufferings are those of childbirth: they bring forth new life. We can all make our own the words of the psalmist: "Yahweh is my strength and my shield...I have been lifted up, my flesh has bloomed again..." (Psalm 28:7). At death, we do not cease to live. We become someone, because Someone is waiting for us. He is already the most intimate friend of those who are sick and dying.

All of being is straining toward an infinite fulfillment. The boldness of our hope measures the quality of our spiritual ideal. And it is in the light of our confidence in a God of love that the permanent renewal of our interior life takes place.

This increase of interior energy expressed in the form of hope will help people who are sick to free themselves from their fears and to abandon themselves to the good will of this ever-present God. Even if they can no longer hope for a cure, they can put their trust in God to support them. Much as a mother holds the hand of her little one in order to walk always further, even so does God lead to where "the new heavens and the new earth" are to be found.

For those who are terminally ill, what consolation there is in the belief that death is a narrow passage opening to their eternal home. If we can imagine and desire eternity, says Saint Augustine, it is because "we carry eternity in the depths of our memory" and we are, therefore, in a certain sense, eternal. "When I will be closer to you than even to myself, there will be no more sorrow for me, no more tiredness. My life, entirely taken up with you, will then be the true Life" (*Confessions* 28:39).

Conclusion

In a society where everything has become oriented toward money and financial gain, and where free services are more and more uncommon, it is marvelous to behold the proliferation of volunteer networks in every area. Visiting and caring for sick people are wonderful acts of mutual aid: these volunteers respond to important needs and bring great joy both to the sick person and to the visiting care-givers.

Education and responsibility

Society has a growing need that relatives, friends and volunteers involve themselves in the comfort and care of those who are sick. In order to be able to offer quality care, however, it is important that these care-givers have a basic knowledge of the psychology of the sick person, of their specific needs at each stage of their illness, and especially of particular difficulties associated with dying.

This practical guide has given an introductory overview of these topics. The readings suggested at the end of each part provide the reader with additional resources for pursuing these questions in more detail.

This increased knowledge, however, will never replace formal qualifications: relatives, friends and volunteers should not undertake medical and paramedical procedures and treatments that ought to be performed by the personnel responsible for care.

The joy of giving and receiving

The ministry of being present with the sick person brings with it many personally satisfying benefits: release from loneliness by reaching out to others, increased self-worth through involvement in practically useful activities, and expansion of all the dimensions of one's being (heart, mind, spirit) through growth in one's availability and freedom.

The joy of those who receive complements the happiness of those who give, and it is impossible to measure which is the greater. The love of the visiting care-givers is manifested in a thousand little gestures, in active listening that validates and frees the other person, in faithful accompaniment during the most difficult moments. This presence is not an inconsiderable factor affecting healing, interior transformation, and the acceptance of the inevitable in peace and, sometimes, in a spirit of deep interior joy.

Suggested readings

Suggested Readings for First Part

Cousins, Norman. *Anatomy of an Illness as Perceived by the Patient*. New York: Bantam, 1981.

Delisle, Isabelle. *Les grands tournants de la vie: L'adaptation au changement*. Montréal: Éditions de Mortagne, 1985.

_____. *À l'écoute de sa vie: Concept santé*. Montréal: Éditions de Mortagne, 1986.

Marrevee, Rev. William. "The Experience of Suffering and Illness: Reflections on the Christian Response" in CHAC REVIEW, Nov/Dec, 1982, vol. 10, no. 6.

Memmi, Albert. *La dépendance*. Paris: Gallimard, 1979.

Oates, Wayne E. *Behind the Masks: Personality Disorders in Religious Behaviour*. Philadelphia: The Westminster Press, 1987.

Peck, Scott. *The Road Less Travelled: A New Psychology of Love. Traditional Values and Spiritual Growth*. New York: Simon and Shuster, 1978.

Sanford, John A. *Healing and Wholeness*. Toronto: Paulist Press, 1966.

Siegel, Bernie S. *Love, Medicine and Miracles: Lessons Learned About Self-Healing From A Surgeon's Experience With Exceptional Patients.* New York: Harper and Row, 1986.

S.I.R.I.M. *Alors survient la maladie.* Paris: Emprika, 1983.

Van Tilburg, MD, Embert. "What is Pain?" in CHAC REVIEW, Sept, 1985, vol. 13, no. 3.

Suggested Readings for Second Part

Baars, Conrad W. *Born Only Once: the miracle of affirmation.* Chicago: Franciscan Herald Press, 1975.

Baars, Conrad W. & Terruwe, Anna A. *Healing the Unaffirmed: recognizing deprivation neurosis.* New York: Alba House, 1976.

Brammer, Lawrence M. *The Helping Relationship: process and skills* (3rd edition). Englewood Cliffs, New Jersey, 1985.

Brody, Jane. *Jane Brody's Nutrition Book: A Lifetime Guide to Good Eating for Better Health and Weight Control by the Personal Health Columnist of The New York Times.* New York: The New York Times Book Co. Inc., 1987.

Kennedy, Eugene C. *On Becoming a Counsellor: a basic guide for non professional counsellors.* New York: Continuum, 1977.

Lapierre-Delisle, Isabelle. *Précis de nutrition.* Montréal: Guérin, 1984.

Lindsay, Anne. *Smart Cooking: Quick and Tasty Recipes for Healthy Living.* Toronto: Macmillan of Canada, 1986.

The Lighthearted Cookbook: Recipes for Healthy Heart Cooking. Toronto: Key Porter Books, 1988.

Robertson, Laurel, et al. *The New Laurel's Kitchen: A Handbook for Vegetarian Cooking and Nutrition.* Berkely, Calif.: Ten Speed Press, 1986.

Suggested Readings for Third Part

Bennett, George. *When the Mental Patient Comes Home.* Philadelphia: The Westminster Press, 1980.

Bernanos, Georges. *The Carmelites.* Translated from the French by Gerard Hopkins. London: Collins (Fontana Books), 1961.

Buscaglia, Leo. *Loving Each Other: The Challenge of Human Relationships.* Toronto: Holt, Rinehart and Winston, Ltd., 1984.

Carkhuff, Robert R. with Richard M. Pierce & John R. Cannon. *The Art of Helping.* (No. IV) Amherst, Mass.: Human Resource Development Press, 1982.

Cassidy, Sheila. *Sharing the Darkness: The Spirituality of Caring.* London: Darton, Longman & Todd Ltd., 1988.

Delisle, Isabelle. *À l'écoute de sa vie.* Montréal: Mortagne, 1986.

_____. *Les grands tournants de la vie.* Montréal: Mortagne, 1985.

_____. *Vivre son mourir: De la relation d'aide aux soins palliatifs.* Montréal: Mortagne, 1982.

Deunov, Peter. *L'amour universel.* Paris: Courrier du livre, 1964.

Doughty, Stephen V. *Ministry of love: a handbook for visiting the aged.* Notre Dame, Ind.: Ave Maria Press, 1984.

Durkenne, Françoise. *Le temps de la bienveillance.* Paris: Médialogue, 1987.

Fromm, Erich. *To Have or To Be?* New York: Harper and Row, 1976.

Grantham, Rudolph E. *Lay Shepherding: A Guide for Visiting the Sick, the Aged, the Troubled, and the Bereaved.* Valley Forge: Judson Press, 1980.

Keys, Joel T. *Our Older Friends: A Guide for Visitors.* Philadelphia: Fortress Press, 1983.

Kübler-Ross, Elizabeth. *AIDS: The Ultimate Challenge.* New York: Macmillan Publishing Co., 1987.

_____. *Death: The Final Stage of Growth.* Englewood Cliffs, N.J.: Prentice-Hall, 1975.

Macdonald, Rev. Bernard A. "To Prolong Life or Let Die," in CHAC REVIEW, Nov/Dec, 1982, vol. 10, no. 6.

Nouwen, Henri J. M. & Gaffney, Walter J. *Aging: the fulfillment of life.* Garden City, New York: Image Books, 1974.

Peel, Donald. *The Ministry of Listening: team visiting in hospital and home.* Toronto: Anglican Book Centre, 1980.

Pope Pius XII. "An Allocution to Physicians," in *Acta Apostolicae Sedis* 49: 1031-32. 1957.

Prigent, Y. *L'expérience dépressive.* Paris: Desclée de Brouwer, 1978.

Reimer, Lawrence D. and James T. Wagner. *The Hospital Handbook: A Practical Guide to Hospital Visitation.* Wilton, Connecticut: Morehouse Barlow, 1984.

Schwartzenberg, L. *Requiem pour la vie.* Le pré aux clercs, 1985.

Valade, Sr. Annette. "Pastoral Care: For the Sick, the Elderly and the Dying," in CHAC REVIEW, June, 1986, vol. 14, no. 2.

Van Bommel, Henry. *Choices for people who have terminal illness, their families and their care-givers.* Toronto: NC Press, 1987.

Westberg, Granger E. *Good Grief: a constructive approach to the problem of loss.* Philadelphia: Fortress Press, 1961.

Suggested Readings for Fourth Part

Bloom, Archbishop Anthony. *Beginning To Pray.* Toronto: Paulist Press, 1970.

Calhoun, Gerald J. *Pastoral Companionship: Ministry with Seriously-Ill Persons and Their Families.* New York: Paulist Press, 1986.

Catoir, John T. *Le Seigneur est ma joie: Vers la contemplation.* Montréal: Éditions Paulines, 1987.

Eaton, Sally. "Spiritual Care: The Software of Life," in *Journal of Palliative Care,* 4:1 & 2, 1988.

Frankl, Viktor. *Man's Search for Meaning.* New York: Pocket Books, 1959, 1980.

Larranaga, Ignace. *Montre-moi ton visage.* Montréal: Éditions Paulines, 1987.

Loup, André. *Spiritual Accompaniment.* Ottawa: Canadian Religious Conference, 1986.

MacNutt, Francis. *The Prayer That Heals: praying for healing in the family.* Notre Dame, Indiana: Ave Maria Press, 1981.

Nouwen, Henri J. M. "Reflections on Compassion," in CHAC REVIEW, July/August (Vol. 8, #4), 1980.

Creative Ministry. Garden City, New York: Image Books, 1978.

The Wounded Healer: Ministry in Contemporary Society. Garden City, New York: Image Books, 1979.

Saunders, Dame Cicely. "Spiritual Pain" in *Journal of Palliative Care* 4:3, 1988.

Tournier, Paul. *A Listening Ear: Reflections on Christian Caring.* Minneapolis: Augsburg Publishing, 1986.

Wolff, Pierre. *May I Hate God?* New York: Paulist Press, 1979.

Glossary
of medical terms

Active Listening: An attitude of welcoming and supportive attention that allows another person to express his or her feelings.

Alopecia: A disease in which a person's hair falls out.

Amnesia: Total or partial loss of memory.

Analgesia: An inability to feel pain.

Anemia: A general or local deficiency in the amount of hemoglobin or the number of red corpuscles in the blood, variously caused, and characterized by pallor, loss of energy, and other symptoms.

Anorexia: A decrease or loss of appetite.

Anxiety: A tense emotional state characterized by an exaggerated fear about a real or fictitious danger.

Aphasia: The absence or impairment of the power of articulate speech, due to a dysfunction of the brain centers.

Authenticity: A strict correspondence between what we think and what we express, between what we are and what we reveal.

Autonomy: The capacity to make one's own decisions and to be self-directing.

Blindness: Partial or total inability to see.

Cachexia: A state of ill health, malnutrition, and wasting, characterized by a waxy or sallow complexion. It may accompany many chronic diseases, certain malignancies, and advanced pulmonary tuberculosis.

Cancer: A malignant tumor that tends to invade surrounding tissue and to spread from one part of the body to another.

Cephalalgia: A headache; a pain in the head.

Chemotherapy: In the treatment of disease, the application of chemical substances that have a toxic effect upon the disease-causing microorganism. It is used to treat cancer.

Coma: A state of unconsciousness from which the person cannot be aroused, even by powerful stimulation. In this condition the person's respiratory, circulatory and eliminatory systems continue to function more or less completely.

Confusion: Not being aware of or oriented with respect to time, place, or self.

Deafness: Partial or total loss of hearing.

Deficiency: Less than the normal amount of elements required for the good functioning of an organism.

Delirium: A state of mental confusion and excitement characterized by disorientation about time and place, usually with illusions and hallucinations.

Dementia: An irrevocable deteriorative mental state with the absence or reduction of intellectual faculties due to organic brain disease.

Empathy: The capacity for participating in or vicariously experiencing another's feelings, volitions or ideas.

Euthanasia: An action or omission of an action which of itself or by intention causes death in order that all suffering may be eliminated.

Incontinence: The inability to retain urine, semen, or feces.

Massage: The action of manipulating the muscles of the body with the hands.

Metastasis: The movement of bacteria or body cells, especially cancer cells, from one part of the body to another. The usual application is to the manifestation of a malignancy as a secondary growth arising from the primary growth in a new location. It is spread by the lymphatics or bloodstream.

Morbid: Diseased.

Necrosis: The death of areas of tissue or bone surrounded by healthy parts.

Neoplasia: A new and abnormal formation of tissue, as a tumor or growth.

Pain: A sensation of discomfort or distress in a part of the body.

Palliative: A treatment serving to relieve or alleviate the symptoms of an illness, without curing the illness.

Paraplegia: Paralysis of the lower portion of the body and of both legs.

Pathology: The branch of medical science that treats of the origin, nature, causes, and development of disease.

Phantasm: An optical illusion; an apparition or illusion of something that does not exist.

Placebo: Inactive pharmaceutical preparations, such as pills, cachets and potions, given for their psychological effect, especially to satisfy a patient's demand for medicine.

Phantasm: An optical illusion; an apparition or illusion of something that does not exist.

Psychotherapy: A method of treating disease, especially nervous disorders, by mental means rather than physical.

Quadriplegia: Paralysis of both arms and both legs.

Radiotherapy: The treatment of disease by application of roentgen rays, radium, ultraviolet and other radiations.

Solicitude: An attitude of concern, opening of the heart, availability and attentive presence.

Stress: The reaction of the body or of the spirit to a new situation, either agreeable or dangerous.

Symptom: Any perceptible change in the body or its functions that indicates the presence of disease.

Therapeutic: Means suitable for healing or relieving sickness.

Sources

Dorland's Illustrated Medical Dictionary. (27th ed.) Philadelphia: W. B. Saunders Co., 1988.

Taber's Cyclopedic Medical Dictionary. Philadelphia: F. A. Davis, Co., 1985.

Thematic Index

It has not been possible to provide a complete index of all the terms used in this book. The selection provided, however, should provide a complementary aid to the Table of Contents.

Achevé d'imprimer
sur les presses de
Les Éditions Marquis
Montmagny (Québec)
en février 1991

Imprimé sur papier alcalin